"50" Paper Hat Patterns

Welcome to
PAPER HAT TRICKS

By Patt Newbold and Anne Diebel

Watch children become excited wearing
PAPER HATS that correlate with:

- science lessons
- animal study units
- reading lessons
- storybook characters
- costumes for plays & skits
- parties
- animal games
- songs or music
- films & filmstrips
- slides or video tapes
- bulletin boards
- reading programs

ACKNOWLEDGMENT

To - Jim Fry - our colleague -
whose expertise and encouragements
were golden.

PAPER HAT TRICKS I. © 1988

Second Printing. 1990
Third Printing. 1991
Fourth Printing. 1992
Fifth Printing. 1993
sixth Printing. 1994
Seventh Printing. 1995
Eighth Printing. 1996

ISBN - 1-56422-999-8

PAPER HAT TRICKS
43546 SERENITY DR.
NORTHVILLE. MI 48167
(810) 349-2560
(517) 529-4343
FAX (810) 349-2560
FAX (517)529-4343

Typeset on a MacIntosh™ computer, with masters printed on an Apple LaserWriter™ Printer by JSF Publishing.

TABLE OF CONTENTS

MATERIALS

- CONSTRUCTION PAPER
- CREPE PAPER
- GUMMED COLORED CIRCLES
- GOLD OR SILVER STARS
- FLAG STICKERS
- SCOTCH TAPE
- SCISSORS
- COTTON BALLS
- NEEDLE & THREAD
- STRING OR YARN
- STAPLER
- PASTE OR GLUE
- CRAYONS
- MAGIC MARKERS
- CHALK
- MIRROR

DIRECTIONS

1. REMOVE PATTERN FROM BOOK WHEN NEEDED.
2. FOLLOW CLEARLY STATED DIRECTIONS ON EACH PATTERN.
3. TRACE PATTERN ONTO TAGBOARD FOR DURABILITY. LABEL PARTS.
4. CUT <u>ALL</u> DOTTED LINES.
5. SOLID LINES ARE FOLDED UNLESS NOTED.
6. CREASE UPRIGHT SHAPES FOR STRENGTH.
7. ALLOW CHILDREN TO TRACE PATTERNS WHEN POSSIBLE.
8. UNLESS OTHERWISE SPECIFIED - USE CONSTRUCTION PAPER FOR ALL HATS. COLORED PAPER IS IMPORTANT FOR HAT'S IMPACT.
9. MAKE MULTIPLE HEADBANDS IN ADVANCE.
10. TEACHER MAY NEED TO CUT OUT MORE COMPLICATED PATTERN PIECES FOR VERY YOUNG CHILDREN.
11. SAVE PATTERN PIECES, DIRECTIONS, & SAMPLE HAT.
12. STORE PATTERNS IN LABELED FILE FOLDERS OR LARGE ENVELOPES.
13. IF TWO OF A PATTERN ARE REQUIRED - PLACE PATTERN ON TWO SHEETS, TRACE ONE, CUT TWO. INCREASE IF NEEDED!

Bibliography
"Great Books for Paper Hats"

Astronaut - "I CAN BE AN ASTRONAUT," June Behrens,
    Childrens Press,1984.

Bat - "HATTIE, THE BACKSTAGE BAT," Don Freeman,
    Puffin, 1988.

Birthday Cake - "A VISIT TO THE BAKERY," R. Ziegler,
    Childrens Press, 1987.

Bunny - "BUNNIES AND THEIR HOBBIES," Nancy Carlson,
    Carolrhoda, 1984.

Butterfly - "JOHNNY AND THE MONARCH," Margaret Friskey,
    Childrens Press, 1984.

Caterpillar - "THE VERY HUNGRY CATERPILLAR," Eric Carle,
    Philomel, 1969.

Chef - "I CAN BE A CHEF," Ann Tomchek, Childrens Press,
    1985.

Colonial Lady - "WHAT'S THE BIG IDEA, BEN FRANKLIN,"
    Jean Fritz, Coward-McCann, 1976.

Deep Sea Diver - "I CAN BE AN OCEANOGRAPHER," Paul
    Sipiera, Childrens Press, 1987.

Dentist - "A TRIP TO THE DENTIST," M. Linn, Harper & Row,
    1988.

Detective - "NATE THE GREAT SERIES," Marjorie Sharmat.

Doctor - "A VISIT TO THE DOCTOR," M. Linn, Harper & Row,
    1988.

Duck - "THE STORY ABOUT PING," Marjorie Flack, Viking, 1933.

Farmer - "WHO TOOK THE FARMER'S HAT?" Joan Nodset,
    Harper, 1963.

Fireman - "FIRE, FIRE!" Gail Gibbons, Crowell, 1984.

Frog - "ONE FROG TOO MANY," Mercer Mayer, Dial, 1975.

George Washington - "MEET GEORGE WASHINGTON,"
    Joan Heilbroner, Random House, 1964.

Hanukkah - "PICTURE BOOK OF HANUKKAH," David Adler,
    Holiday House,1982.

King/Queen - "KING'S STILTS," Dr. Seuss, Random House, 1967.

Nurse - "CURIOUS GEORGE GOES TO THE HOSPITAL,"
    Margaret Rey, Houghton Mifflin, 1966.

Pilgrim Lady - "THANKSGIVING DAY," Gail Gibbons, Holiday
    House, 1983.

Pilgrim Man - "BEST THANKSGIVING BOOKS," Pat Whitehead,
    Troll, 1985.

Pioneer Woman - "CASSIE'S JOURNEY," Brett Harvey,
    Holiday House, 1988.

Policeman - "POLICE," Ray Broekel, Childrens Press, 1981.

Rabbit - "RABBIT'S MORNING," Nancy Tafuri, Greenwillow,
    1985.

Reindeer - "RUDOLF, THE RED-NOSED REINDEER," Barbara
    Hazen, Golden Press, 1958.

Robin Hood - "ROBIN HOOD STORIES," Edward Dolch, Garrard,
    1957.

Santa Claus - "SANTA'S CRASH-BANG CHRISTMAS," Steven
    Kroll, Holiday House, 1982.

Spider - "THE VERY BUSY SPIDER," Eric Carle, Philomel, 1984.

Statue of Liberty - "STORY OF THE STATUE OF LIBERTY,"
    B. Maestro, Lothrop, Lee, 1986.

Teddy Bear - "RUNAWAY TEDDY BEAR," Ginnie Hofman,
    Random House, 1986.

Train Engineer - "TRAINS," Gail Gibbons, Holiday House, 1987.

1. CUT OUT PATTERN & CENTER.
2. TRACE ON GRAY OR WHITE PAPER, CUT OUT.
3. PRINT U.S.A. ON LOWER CORNER.
4. PUT FLAG STICKER ON OPPOSITE SIDE.
5. DRAW CIRCLES & LINES AS SHOWN.
6. STAPLE SIDES TO 3" HEADBAND, FIT TO HEAD.
7. 3-2-1 "BLAST OFF!
8. RACE CAR DRIVER HELMET COULD HAVE DESIGNS OF TIRES, OIL CANS, ETC ON SIDES. HELMET COULD BE RED OR YELLOW.

ASTRONAUT HAT

- **Race Car Driver**

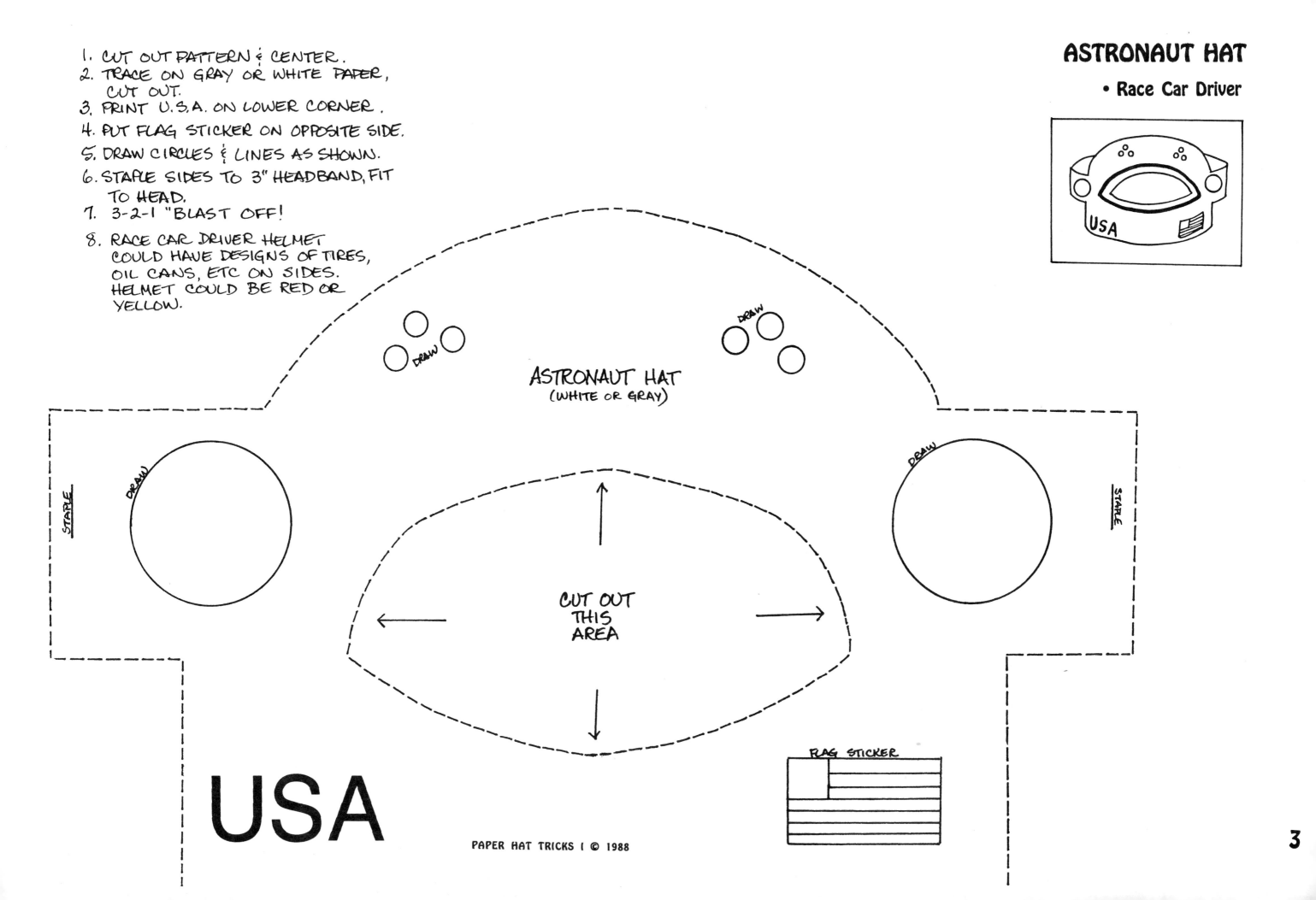

ASTRONAUT HAT
(WHITE OR GRAY)

DRAW

DRAW

STAPLE

DRAW

DRAW

STAPLE

CUT OUT THIS AREA

USA

FLAG STICKER

PAPER HAT TRICKS I © 1988

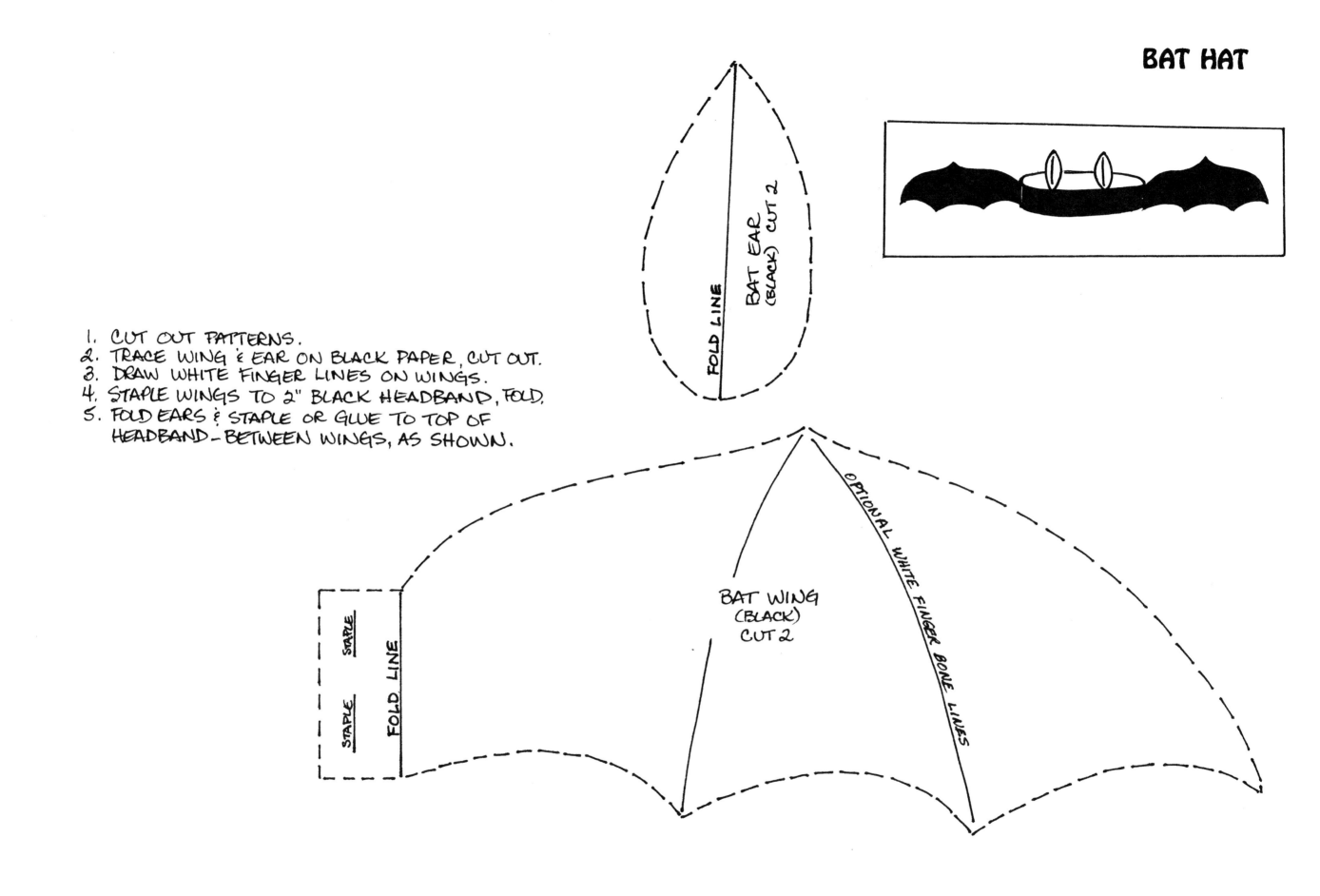

1. CUT OUT PATTERNS.
2. TRACE WING & EAR ON BLACK PAPER, CUT OUT.
3. DRAW WHITE FINGER LINES ON WINGS.
4. STAPLE WINGS TO 2" BLACK HEADBAND, FOLD.
5. FOLD EARS & STAPLE OR GLUE TO TOP OF HEADBAND — BETWEEN WINGS, AS SHOWN.

FOLD LINE

BAT EAR (BLACK) CUT 2

STAPLE

STAPLE

FOLD LINE

BAT WING (BLACK) CUT 2

OPTIONAL WHITE FINGER BONE LINES

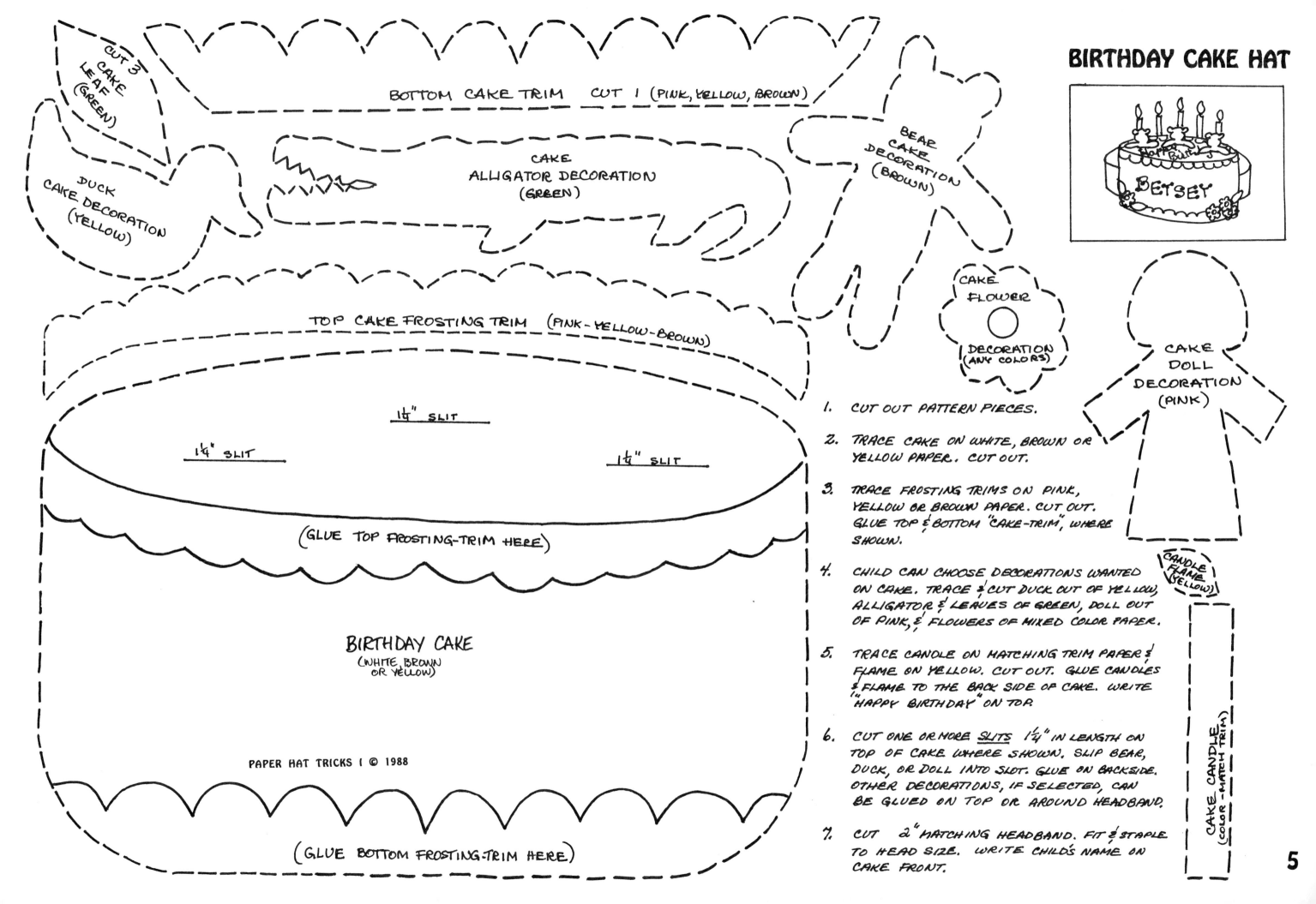

CUT 3
CAKE
LEAF
(GREEN)

BOTTOM CAKE TRIM   CUT 1 (PINK, YELLOW, BROWN)

BIRTHDAY CAKE HAT

CAKE
ALLIGATOR DECORATION
(GREEN)

BEAR
CAKE
DECORATION
(BROWN)

DUCK
CAKE DECORATION
(YELLOW)

CAKE
FLOWER

DECORATION
(ANY COLORS)

CAKE
DOLL
DECORATION
(PINK)

TOP CAKE FROSTING TRIM   (PINK - YELLOW - BROWN)

1¼" SLIT

1¼" SLIT

1¼" SLIT

(GLUE TOP FROSTING-TRIM HERE)

1. CUT OUT PATTERN PIECES.

2. TRACE CAKE ON WHITE, BROWN OR YELLOW PAPER. CUT OUT.

3. TRACE FROSTING TRIMS ON PINK, YELLOW OR BROWN PAPER. CUT OUT. GLUE TOP & BOTTOM "CAKE-TRIM" WHERE SHOWN.

4. CHILD CAN CHOOSE DECORATIONS WANTED ON CAKE. TRACE & CUT DUCK OUT OF YELLOW, ALLIGATOR & LEAVES OF GREEN, DOLL OUT OF PINK, & FLOWERS OF MIXED COLOR PAPER.

5. TRACE CANDLE ON MATCHING TRIM PAPER & FLAME ON YELLOW. CUT OUT. GLUE CANDLES & FLAME TO THE BACK SIDE OF CAKE. WRITE "HAPPY BIRTHDAY" ON TOP.

BIRTHDAY CAKE
(WHITE, BROWN OR YELLOW)

PAPER HAT TRICKS I © 1988

CANDLE FLAME (YELLOW)

CAKE CANDLE (COLOR - MATCH TRIM)

6. CUT ONE OR MORE SLITS 1¼" IN LENGTH ON TOP OF CAKE WHERE SHOWN. SLIP BEAR, DUCK, OR DOLL INTO SLOT. GLUE ON BACKSIDE. OTHER DECORATIONS, IF SELECTED, CAN BE GLUED ON TOP OR AROUND HEADBAND.

7. CUT 2" MATCHING HEADBAND. FIT & STAPLE TO HEAD SIZE. WRITE CHILD'S NAME ON CAKE FRONT.

(GLUE BOTTOM FROSTING-TRIM HERE)

5

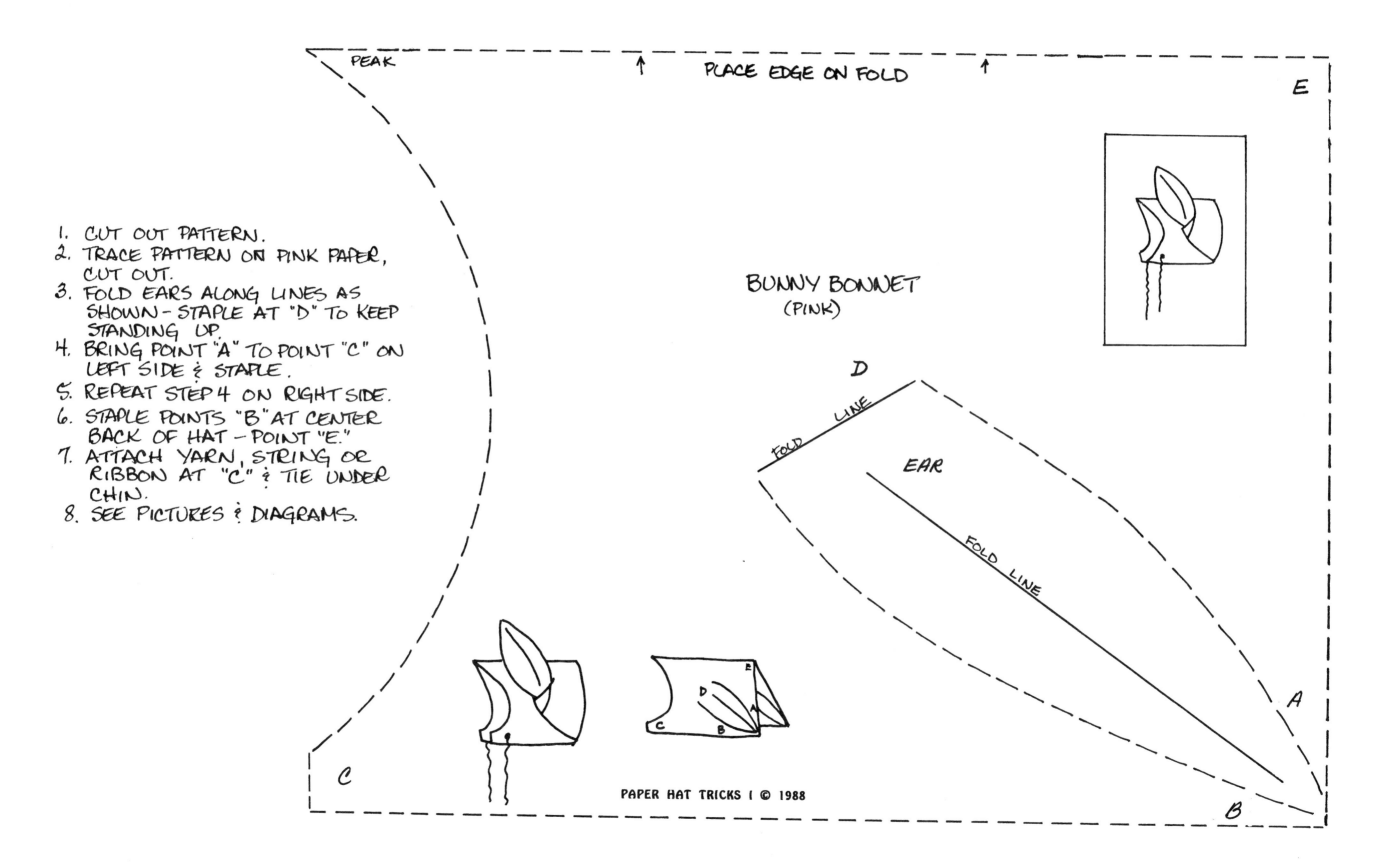

PEAK

↑ PLACE EDGE ON FOLD ↑

E

BUNNY BONNET
(PINK)

1. CUT OUT PATTERN.
2. TRACE PATTERN ON PINK PAPER, CUT OUT.
3. FOLD EARS ALONG LINES AS SHOWN - STAPLE AT "D" TO KEEP STANDING UP.
4. BRING POINT "A" TO POINT "C" ON LEFT SIDE & STAPLE.
5. REPEAT STEP 4 ON RIGHT SIDE.
6. STAPLE POINTS "B" AT CENTER BACK OF HAT — POINT "E."
7. ATTACH YARN, STRING OR RIBBON AT "C" & TIE UNDER CHIN.
8. SEE PICTURES & DIAGRAMS.

D

FOLD LINE

FOLD LINE

EAR

A

C

B

PAPER HAT TRICKS I © 1988

6

BUTTERFLY HAT

BUTTERFLY SPOT #1
(ORANGE)
CUT 2

BUTTERFLY SPOT #4
(ORANGE)
CUT 2

BUTTERFLY SPOT #3
(ORANGE)
CUT 2

BUTTERFLY SPOT #2
(ORANGE)
CUT 2

BUTTERFLY ANTENNA
(BLACK)
CUT 2

GLUE SPOT #1
HERE

GLUE SPOT #2
HERE

GLUE SPOT #3
HERE

GLUE SPOT #4
HERE

BUTTERFLY
(BLACK)
CUT 2

FOLD LINE

STAPLE

STAPLE

WHITE DOTS

1. CUT OUT PATTERNS.
2. TRACE WING & ANTENNA ON BLACK PAPER, CUT OUT — 2.
3. TRACE NUMBERED SHAPES ON ORANGE PAPER, CUT OUT — 2 OF EACH.
4. GLUE ORANGE SHAPES ON WINGS AS SHOWN.
5. COLOR WHITE DOTS ON WINGS AS SHOWN OR USE WHITE DOTS.
6. FOLD WINGS ON LINE & STAPLE TO 2"X24" BLACK HEADBAND — FIT TO HEAD.
7. GLUE ANTENNA TO TOP OF HEADBAND IN FRONT BETWEEN WINGS & CURL FORWARD.

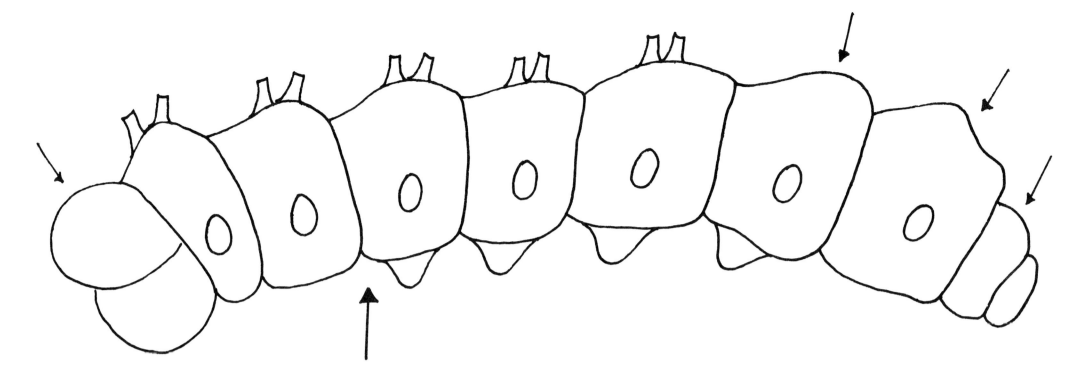

CATERPILLAR HAT - CECROPIA MOTH LARVA

1. MAKE COPIES OF CATERPILLAR ON PALE GREEN PAPER.

2. COLOR OVAL AREAS & PROTRUSIONS ON TOP YELLOW.

3. TRACE ANTENNA ON BROWN PAPER, CUT OUT. GLUE AT ARROWS AS SHOWN.

4. STAPLE TO BACK OF CECROPIA MOTH HAT TO SHOW TWO STAGES OF DEVELOPMENT.

MOTH ANTENNA (BROWN) CUT 4

CATERPILLAR HAT - MONARCH LARVA

1. MAKE COPIES OF CATERPILLAR. CUT OUT. COLOR: B- BLACK, O- ORANGE, LEAVE W- WHITE.

2. TRACE ANTENNA ON BLACK PAPER, CUT OUT. CURL ENDS. GLUE 2 AT EACH ARROW.

3. STAPLE TO 2" BLACK HEADBAND. FIT TO HEAD.

4. MAY BE STAPLED TO BACK OF BUTTERFLY HAT (SEE "PAPER HAT TRICKS I") TO SHOW 2 STAGES OF DEVELOPMENT.

CUT 4   CATERPILLAR ANTENNA   (BLACK)

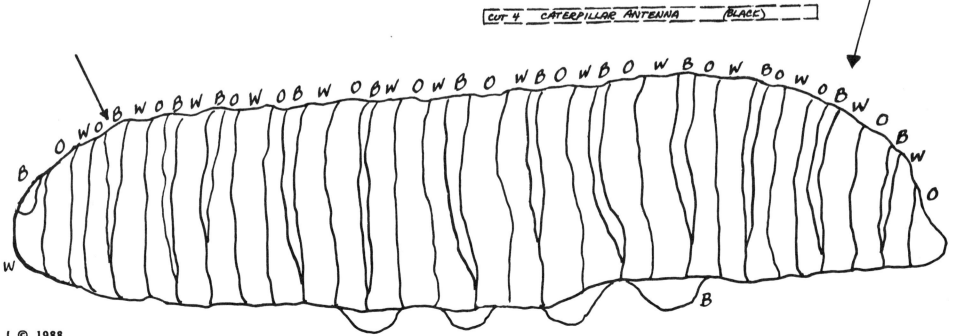

1. CUT 2 HEADBANDS 4"x12" OUT OF WHITE PAPER, FIT TO HEAD.
2. PRINT NAME ON HEADBAND WITH "CHEF" ABOVE AS SHOWN.
3. TUCK CORNERS OF LARGE WHITE DINNER NAPKIN EVENLY AROUND HEADBAND. STAPLE CORNERS.
4. PUFF TOP OF NAPKIN AS HIGH AS POSSIBLE.
5. WHITE CREPE PAPER CUT IN 16" SQUARES CAN BE USED INSTEAD OF NAPKINS.
6. CAN DECORATE HEADBAND TO MAKE MORE ATTRACTIVE.

CHEF SUSIE

CHEF HAT
(WHITE)
CUT 2

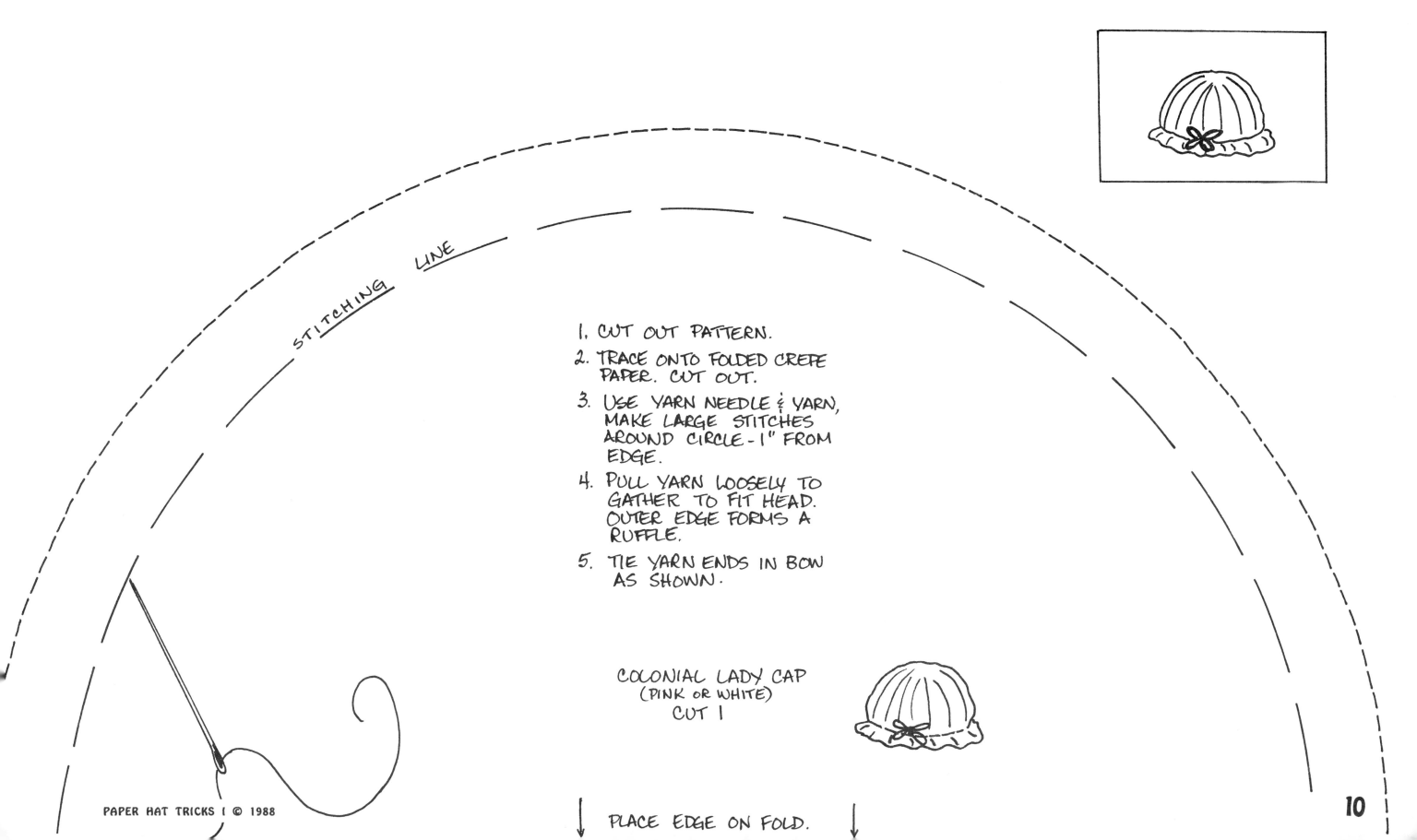

STITCHING LINE

1. CUT OUT PATTERN.

2. TRACE ONTO FOLDED CREPE PAPER. CUT OUT.

3. USE YARN NEEDLE & YARN, MAKE LARGE STITCHES AROUND CIRCLE - 1" FROM EDGE.

4. PULL YARN LOOSELY TO GATHER TO FIT HEAD. OUTER EDGE FORMS A RUFFLE.

5. TIE YARN ENDS IN BOW AS SHOWN.

COLONIAL LADY CAP
(PINK OR WHITE)
CUT 1

↓ PLACE EDGE ON FOLD. ↓

C.

DRAW LINE

DRAW LINE

DRAW LINE

DRAW LINES

DRAW LINES

B.

DRAW LINE

A.

DRAW LINE

CUT OUT CENTER

DEEP SEA DIVER HELMET
(GRAY)

DRAW LINE

DEEP SEA DIVER HELMET

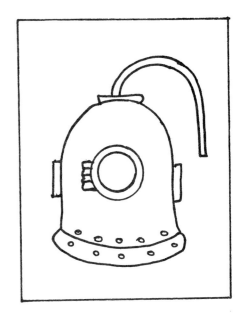

1. CUT OUT PATTERN.
2. TRACE PATTER ON GRAY PAPER. CUT OUT.
3. DRAW DETAILS ON HAT AS SHOWN. USE WHITE DOTS FOR RIVETS OR DRAW THEM.
4. STAPLE 2" HEADBAND AT "A." FIT TO HEAD. STAPLE AT "B."
5. CUT STRIP OF BLACK PAPER 2" X 18." STAPLE ONE END AT "C" LET OTHER END HANG — THIS IS AIR HOSE.

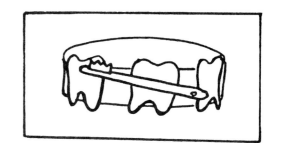

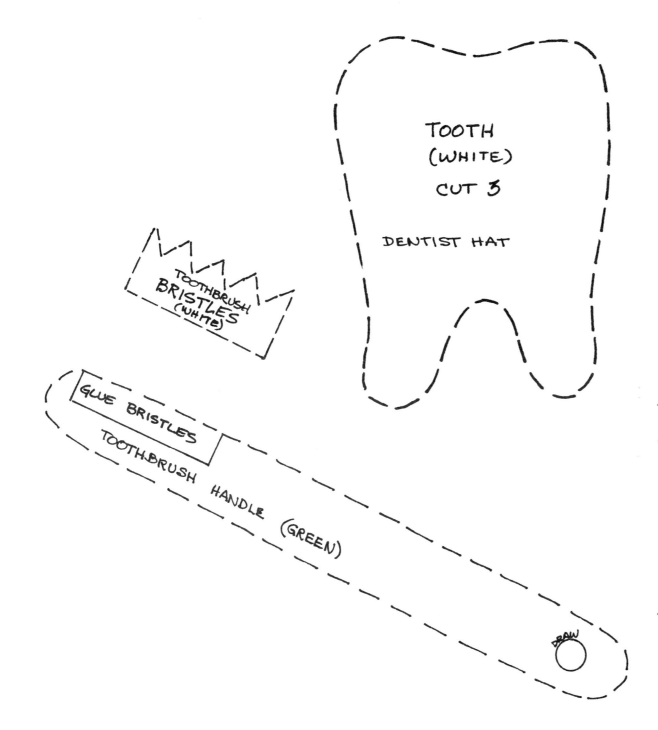

TOOTH
(WHITE)

CUT 3

DENTIST HAT

TOOTHBRUSH
BRISTLES
(WHITE)

GLUE BRISTLES

TOOTHBRUSH HANDLE (GREEN)

DRAIN

1. CUT OUT PATTERNS.

2. MAKE 2" PINK HEADBAND.

3. TRACE TOOTH ON WHITE PAPER CUT OUT 3 TEETH.

4. TRACE TOOTHBRUSH BRISTLES ON WHITE PAPER AND HANDLE ON GREEN PAPER. CUT OUT. GLUE TEETH ON HEADBAND AS SHOWN. GLUE BRUSH ON BAND.

5. FIT HEADBAND TO HEAD SIZE.

CUT OUT
PUT CLEAR PLASTIC
HERE TO SEE
THROUGH

MAGNIFING GLASS
(BROWN)

DETECTIVE - SHERLOCK HOLMES HAT

COLOR BLACK

DRAW LINES

DETECTIVE HAT
(BROWN)

STAPLE

STAPLE

1. CUT OUT PATTERNS.
2. TRACE PATTERNS ON BROWN PAPER, CUT OUT.
3. DRAW LINES & OUTLINE HAT AS SHOWN, GLASS, TOO.
4. STAPLE HAT TO 2" BROWN HEADBAND.

DOCTOR HAT

1. CUT OUT PATTERNS.
2. TRACE CIRCLE ON GRAY PAPER, CUT OUT.
3. PUT BLACK & WHITE DOTS IN CENTER AS SHOWN.
4. GLUE CIRCLE TO HEADBAND AS SHOWN. FIT TO HEAD.
5. TRACE STETHOSCOPE ON BLACK PAPER, CUT OUT.
6. COLOR ENDS AS SHOWN. HANG AROUND NECK.

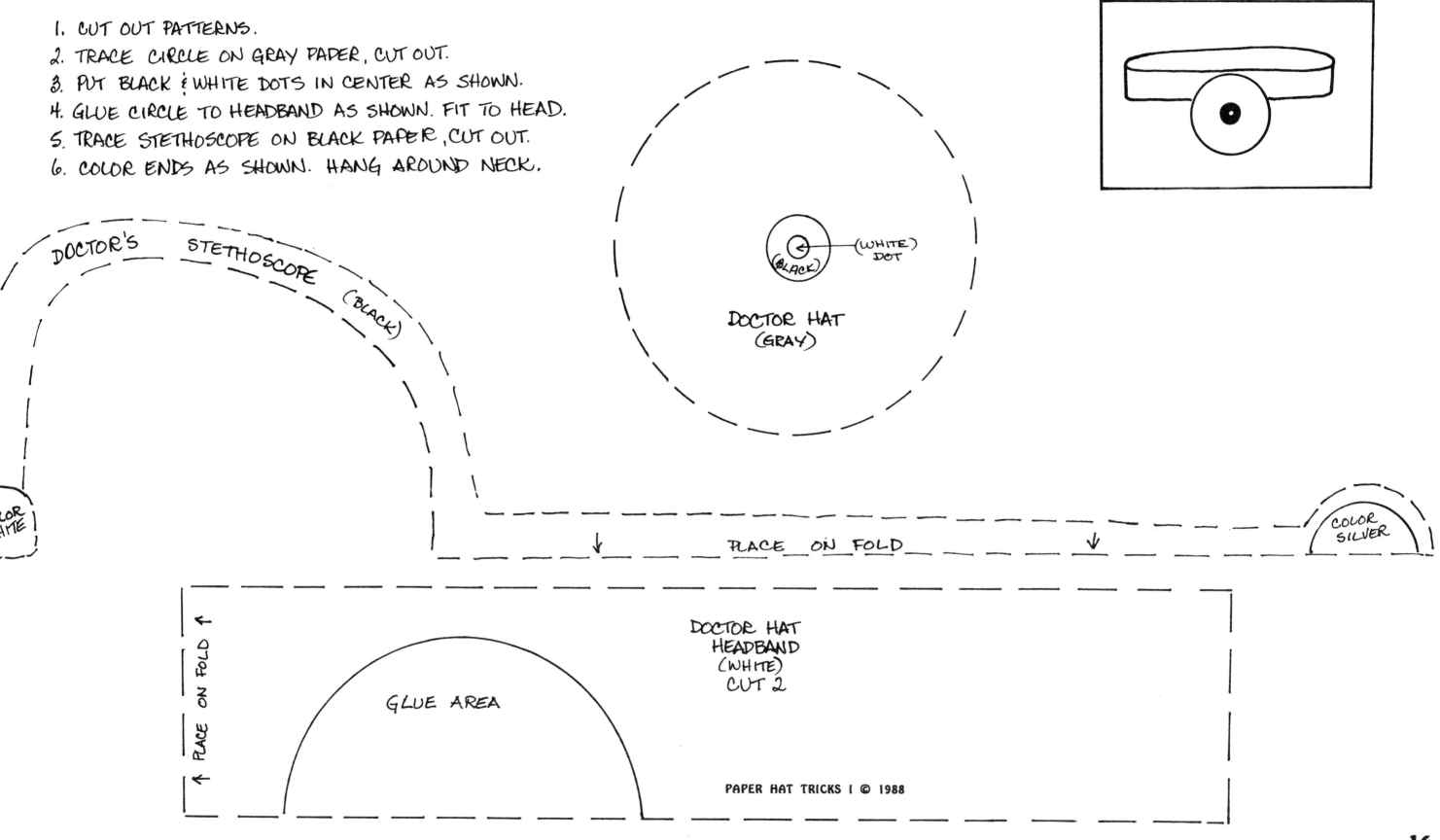

DOCTOR'S STETHOSCOPE (BLACK)

COLOR WHITE

(BLACK) (WHITE) DOT

DOCTOR HAT (GRAY)

COLOR SILVER

PLACE ON FOLD

PLACE ON FOLD

GLUE AREA

DOCTOR HAT HEADBAND (WHITE) CUT 2

PAPER HAT TRICKS I © 1988

14

STAPLE

STAPLE

FOLD LINE

DUCK BILL
(ORANGE)
CUT 2

DUCK WING
(YELLOW)
CUT 2

FOLD LINE

STAPLE

1. CUT OUT PATTERNS.

2. TRACE BILL ON ORANGE PAPER, CUT OUT.
   FOLD ALONG LINE AS SHOWN.

3. TRACE WINGS ON YELLOW PAPER, CUT OUT.
   FOLD ALONG LINE AS SHOWN.

4. STAPLE BILLS TO 3" YELLOW HEADBAND.
   FIT TO HEAD.

5. STAPLE WINGS ON SIDES, AS SHOWN.

6. ADD WHITE & BLUE DOTS FOR EYES.

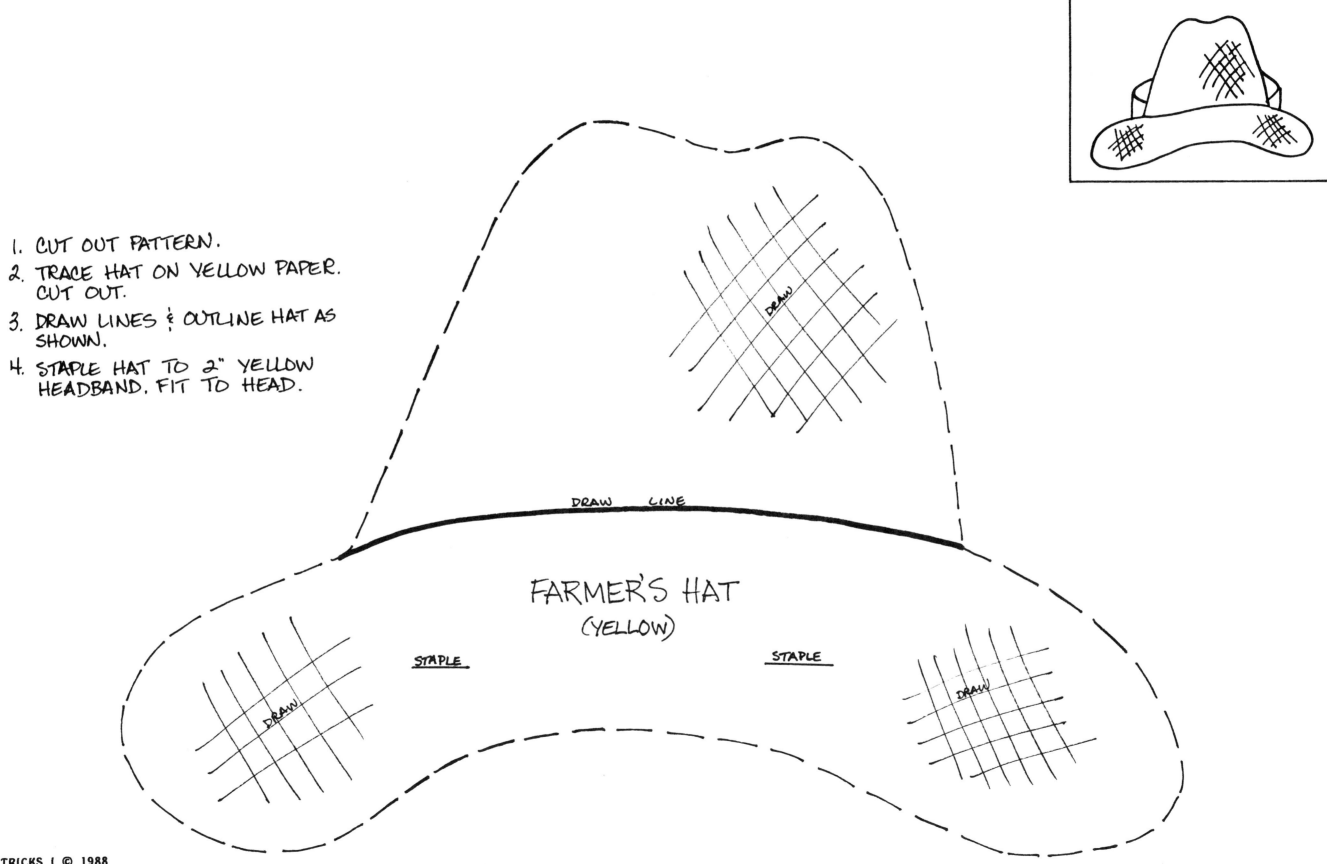

1. CUT OUT PATTERN.
2. TRACE HAT ON YELLOW PAPER. CUT OUT.
3. DRAW LINES & OUTLINE HAT AS SHOWN.
4. STAPLE HAT TO 2" YELLOW HEADBAND. FIT TO HEAD.

DRAW LINE

FARMER'S HAT
(YELLOW)

STAPLE   STAPLE

DRAW

DRAW

DRAW

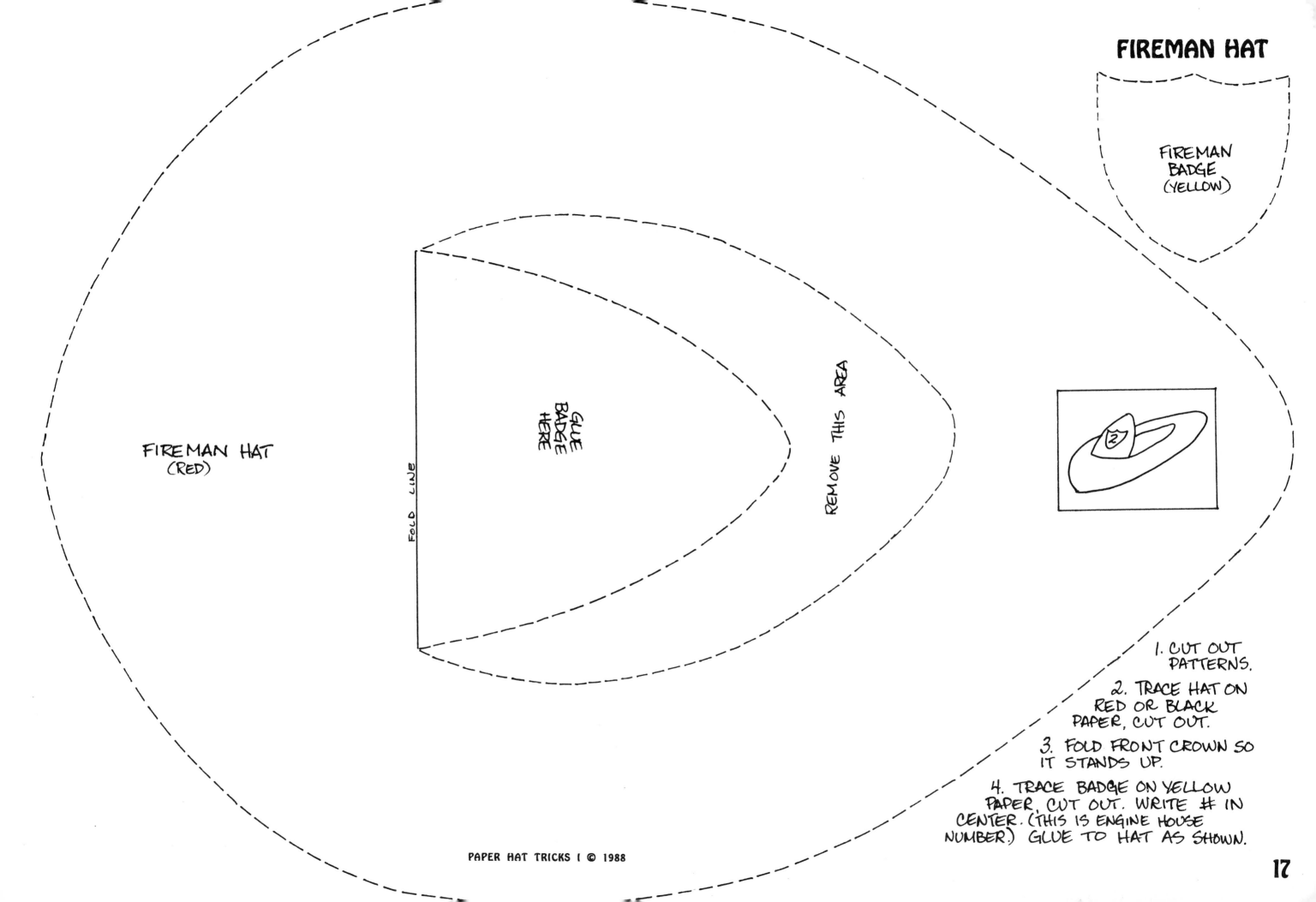

FIREMAN HAT

FIREMAN
BADGE
(YELLOW)

FIREMAN HAT
(RED)

FOLD LINE

GLUE
BADGE
HERE

REMOVE THIS AREA

1. CUT OUT
PATTERNS.

2. TRACE HAT ON
RED OR BLACK
PAPER, CUT OUT.

3. FOLD FRONT CROWN SO
IT STANDS UP.

4. TRACE BADGE ON YELLOW
PAPER, CUT OUT. WRITE # IN
CENTER. (THIS IS ENGINE HOUSE
NUMBER.) GLUE TO HAT AS SHOWN.

FROG HAT

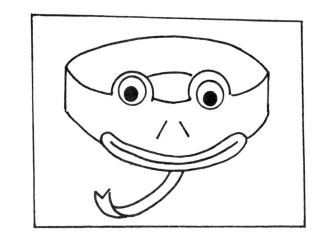

1. CUT OUT PATTERNS.
2. TRACE HEAD ON GREEN PAPER. CUT OUT.
3. PUT DOTS FOR EYES. DRAW LINES FOR MOUTH AS SHOWN.
4. TRACE TONGUE ON PINK PAPER. CUT OUT. CURL "A" END. GLUE "B" END UNDER MOUTH AS SHOWN.
5. CUT 2"X12" GREEN HEADBAND - STAPLE TO HAT AT "C" & "D."

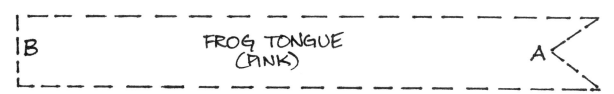

B
FROG TONGUE
(PINK)
A

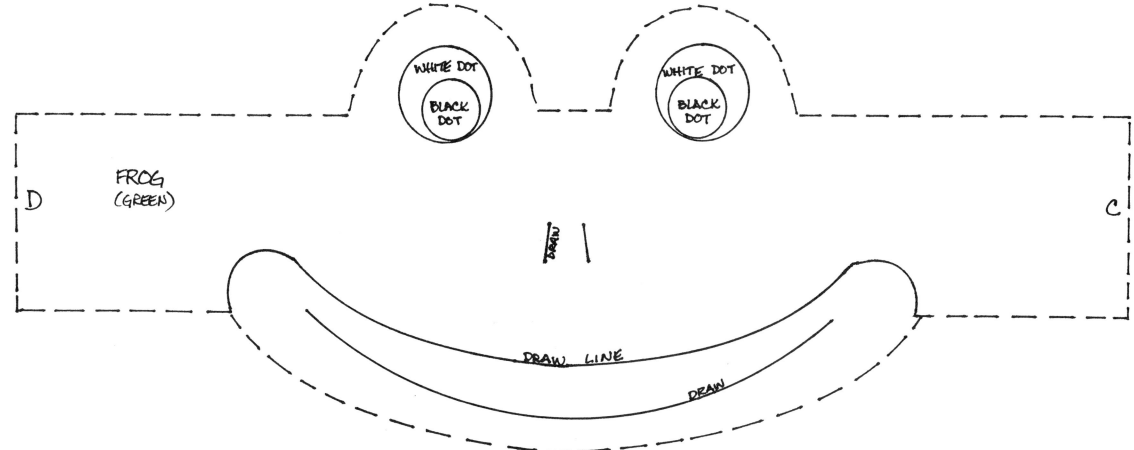

WHITE DOT
BLACK DOT

WHITE DOT
BLACK DOT

D
FROG
(GREEN)
C

DRAW

DRAW LINE

DRAW

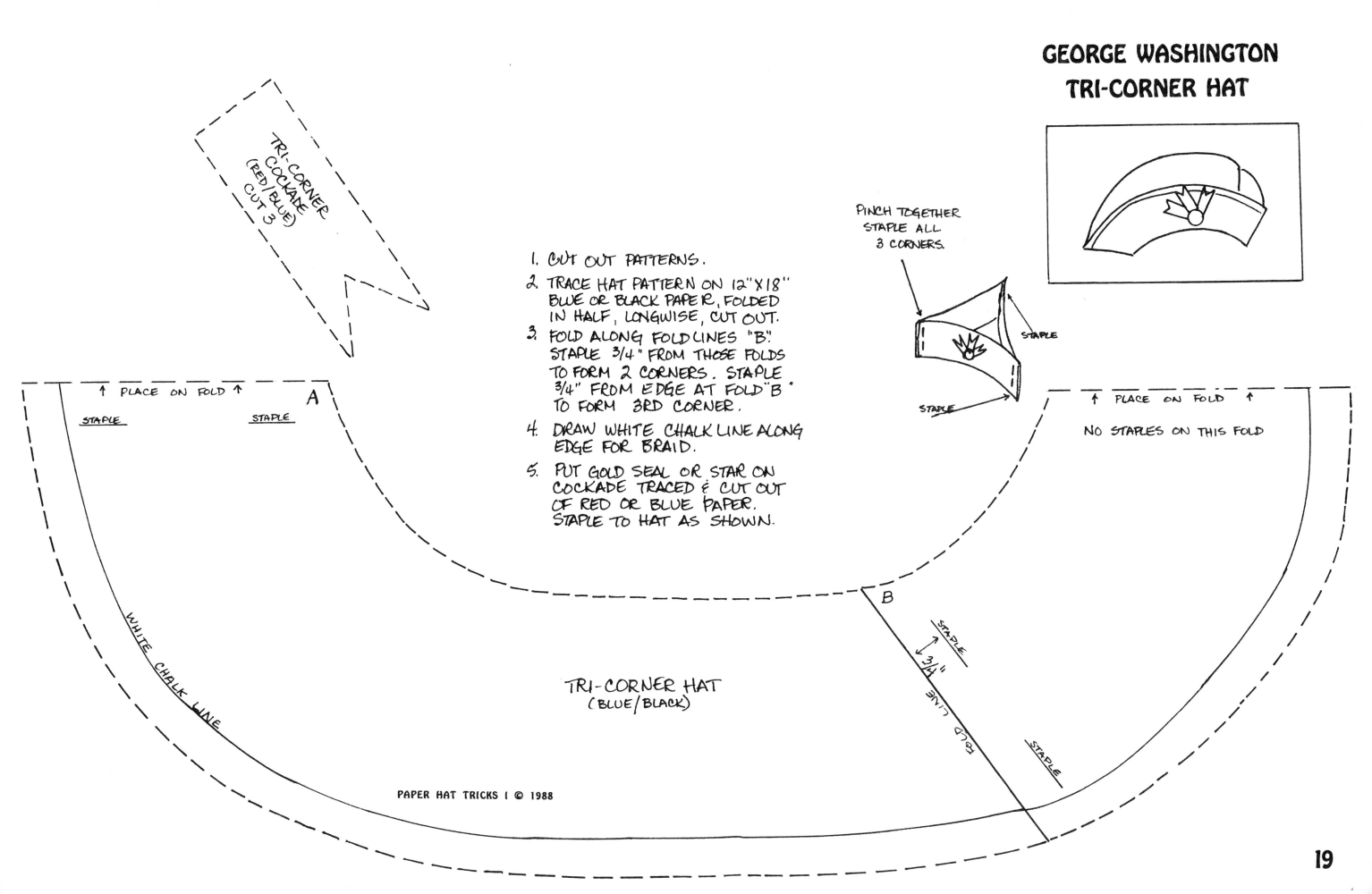

GEORGE WASHINGTON TRI-CORNER HAT

TRI-CORNER COCKADE (RED/BLUE) CUT 3

PINCH TOGETHER STAPLE ALL 3 CORNERS.

STAPLE

STAPLE

1. CUT OUT PATTERNS.

2. TRACE HAT PATTERN ON 12"X18" BLUE OR BLACK PAPER, FOLDED IN HALF, LONGWISE, CUT OUT.

3. FOLD ALONG FOLD LINES "B". STAPLE 3/4" FROM THOSE FOLDS TO FORM 2 CORNERS. STAPLE 3/4" FROM EDGE AT FOLD "B" TO FORM 3RD CORNER.

4. DRAW WHITE CHALK LINE ALONG EDGE FOR BRAID.

5. PUT GOLD SEAL OR STAR ON COCKADE TRACED & CUT OUT OF RED OR BLUE PAPER. STAPLE TO HAT AS SHOWN.

↑ PLACE ON FOLD ↑   A

STAPLE   STAPLE

↑ PLACE ON FOLD ↑

NO STAPLES ON THIS FOLD

WHITE CHALK LINE

B

STAPLE

3/4"

FOLD LINE

STAPLE

TRI-CORNER HAT
(BLUE/BLACK)

PAPER HAT TRICKS I © 1988

19

1. CUT OUT PATTERN.
2. TRACE ON BLACK PAPER, CUT 2.
3. STAPLE ENDS TO MAKE LONG STRIP.
4. FOLD ALONG FOLD LINES. CUT TO FOLD LINES AT INTERVALS AS SHOWN. (DIAGRAM 1)
5. FIT TO HEAD & STAPLE OTHER ENDS. POINT SHOULD BE OVER FOREHEAD.
6. FOLD CUT PIECES INWARD. (DIAGRAM 2)
7. TURN UPSIDE DOWN & PLACE HEAD-BAND UNIT IN CENTER OF 9"X9" PAPER OF SAME COLOR.
8. TAPE OR GLUE HEADBAND UNIT TO SQUARE.
9. ADD TASSEL MADE OF YARN TO CENTER OF HAT—USE PAPER FASTENER.

DIAGRAM 2

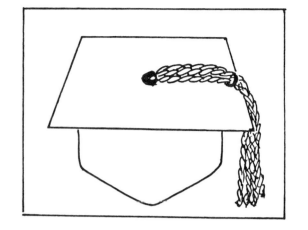

cut lines

DIAGRAM 1

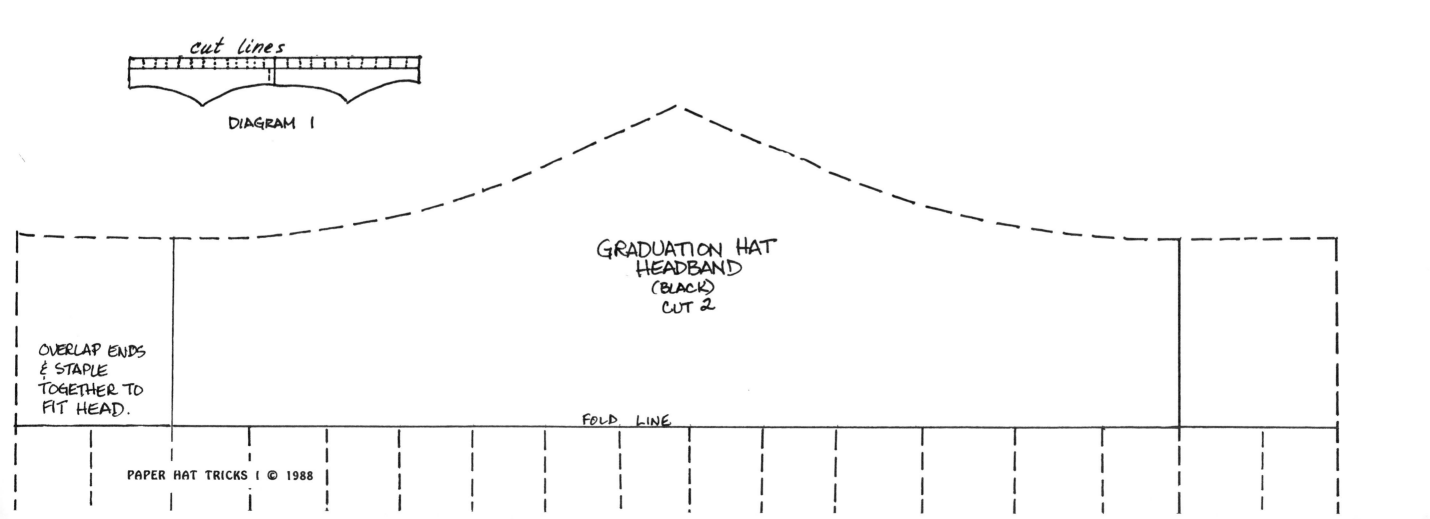

GRADUATION HAT
HEADBAND
(BLACK)
CUT 2

OVERLAP ENDS & STAPLE TOGETHER TO FIT HEAD.

FOLD LINE

1. CUT OUT PATTERNS.
2. TRACE HAT ON GRAY PAPER, CUT OUT.
3. WRITE "HAPPY HANUKKAH" ON HAT.
4. STAPLE 2" x 12" HEADBAND TO "B." FIT TO HEAD, STAPLE TO "A."
5. TRACE FLAME ON YELLOW PAPER. CUT 9.
6. GLUE ONE FLAME EACH DAY OF HANUKKAH.

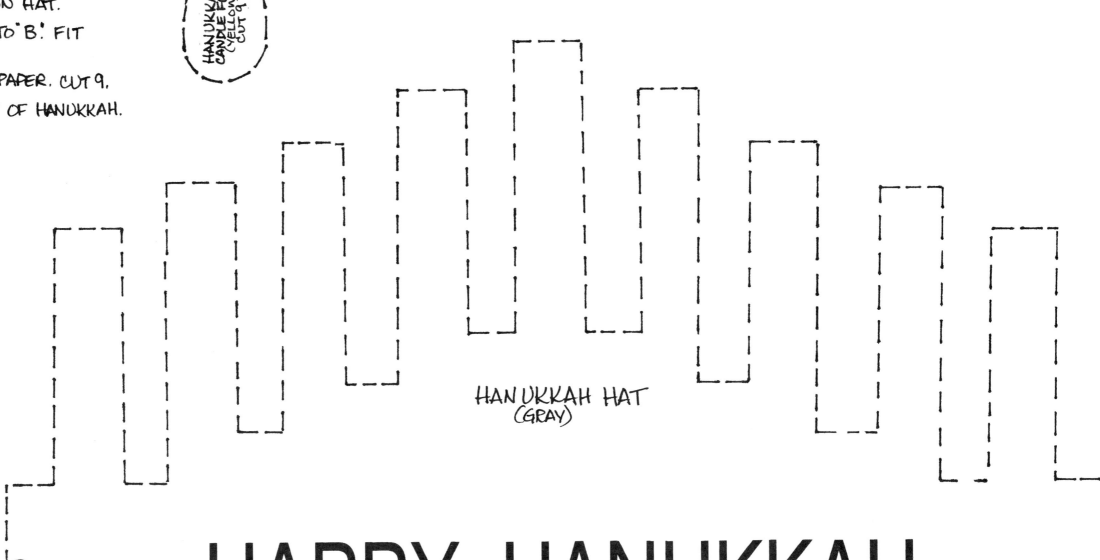

HANUKKAH CANDLE FLAME (YELLOW) CUT 9

HANUKKAH HAT (GRAY)

B.

A.

HAPPY HANUKKAH

PAPER HAT TRICKS I © 1988

21

KING AND QUEEN CROWNS

- Prince
- Princess

KING'S CROWN
(PURPLE)
CUT 1
PATTERN # 1

STAR FOR WAND
(YELLOW)

1. CUT OUT PATTERNS.
2. TRACE QUEEN'S CROWN ON GOLD PAPER. CUT OUT.
3. TRACE KING'S CROWN ON PURPLE PAPER. CUT OUT.
4. CUT 1⅜" HEADBAND OF MATCHING COLOR. STAPLE TO ONE END, FIT TO HEAD. STAPLE OTHER END.
5. DECORATE WITH GLITTER, SEALS, DOTS, OR CRAYONS OR MARKERS.
6. CROWN CAN BE USED FOR CINDERELLA'S FAIRY GODMOTHER. USE STAR TO MAKE MAGIC WAND.

← PLACE ON FOLD →

QUEEN'S CROWN
(GOLD)
CUT 1
PATTERN # 2

PAPER HAT TRICKS I © 1988

NURSE CAP

• Waitress

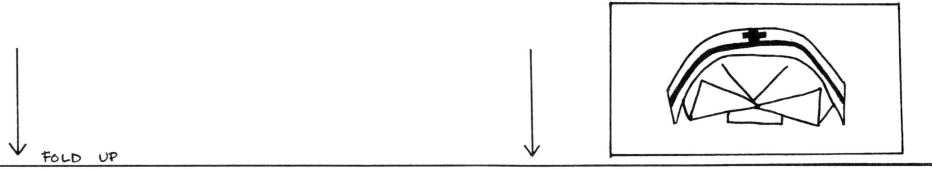

FOLD UP

1. CUT OUT PATTERNS.
2. TRACE HAT ON WHITE PAPER. CUT OUT.
3. CUT FROM POINTS "A" TO "C".
4. FOLD UP CORNERS ALONG FOLD LINES.
5. TAKE POINT "A" ON EACH SIDE & OVERLAP POINTS SLIGHTLY. HOLD TOGETHER & STAPLE TO POINT "B" AS INDICATED.

6. FOLD LONGEST FOLD LINE FOR BRIM OF CAP.
7. GLUE 1" STRIP OF BLACK PAPER ACROSS BRIM ABOUT AN 1" FROM EDGE.
8. GLUE RED CROSS ON CENTER OF BRIM AS SHOWN.

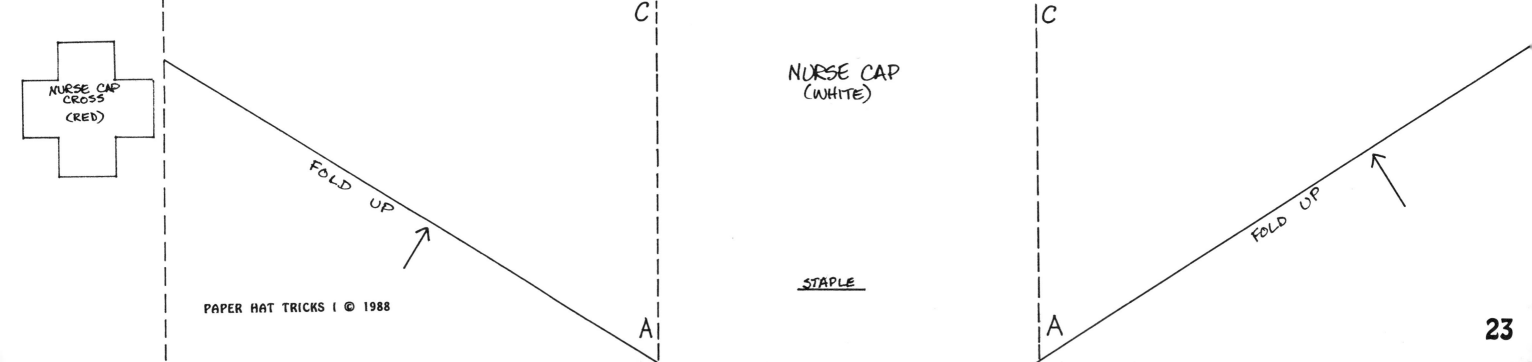

NURSE CAP CROSS (RED)

C

NURSE CAP (WHITE)

C

FOLD UP

FOLD UP

STAPLE

A

A

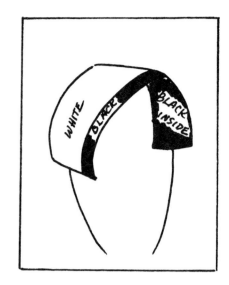

PILGRIM LADY HAT
BOTTOM
(BLACK)

1. CUT OUT PATTERNS.

2. TRACE ON WHITE & BLACK PAPER. CUT OUT.

3. GLUE WHITE PART ON TOP OF BLACK PART. LEAVE 3/4" BAND OF BLACK ON LONG SIDE.

4. FOLD THIS 3/4" BAND OF BLACK OVER TOP OF WHITE.

5. STAPLE PIECES OF YARN OR STRING IN CENTER OF EACH END, AS SHOWN.

PILGRIM LADY HAT
TOP
(WHITE)

1. CUT OUT PATTERNS.

2. TRACE HAT ON FOLDED BLACK PAPER.
   CUT OUT - DIAGRAM #1.

3. OPEN HAT & FOLD CROWN FORWARD
   TO MAKE CENTER STAND-UP.

4. TRACE BUCKLE ON YELLOW PAPER.
   CUT OUT.

5. GLUE BUCKLE TO CENTER OF HAT
   AS SHOWN.

PILGRIM MAN HAT

- Abe Lincoln Hat
- Magician Hat
- Frosty Snowman Hat

CUT OUT

CUT OUT

PILGRIM MAN HAT
BUCKLE
(YELLOW)

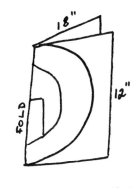

18"

12"

FOLD

DIAGRAM #1

PILGRIM MAN HAT
(BLACK)

GLUE YELLOW
BUCKLE HERE

FOLD UP

PLACE ON FOLD

PLACE ON FOLD

PIONEER WOMAN HAT

• Sunbonnet

THIS IS "NOT" A CUT LINE!
STAPLE CREPE PAPER ALONG THIS EDGE UNDERNEATH, GATHERING ALONG THE EDGE. RAW EDGE INSIDE HAT.

STAPLE STRING HERE

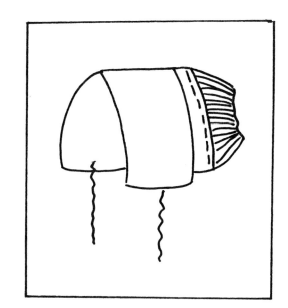

PIONEER WOMAN HAT
(PINK)

FOLD UP & OVER

1. ENTIRE PAGE IS PATTERN.

2. TRACE ON PINK PAPER.

3. FOLD BRIM OVER.

4. CUT STRIP OF PINK CREPE PAPER 8" X 34."

5. GATHER & STAPLE EDGE OF CREPE PAPER TO EDGE OF PATTERN AS SHOWN.

6. GATHER OTHER EDGE OF CREPE PAPER INTO SMALL BUNCH & FLATTEN. STAPLE TOGETHER.

7. ATTACH STRING OR YARN PIECES TO EACH SIDE. TIE UNDER CHIN AS SHOWN.

8. NOTE: BONNET CAN BE MADE OF SMALL PATTERNED WALLPAPER TO LOOK LIKE CALICO.

POLICEMAN HAT
(BLUE)
PATTERN "A"
CUT 1

- Bus Driver
- Mailman
- Soldier

DRAW LINE

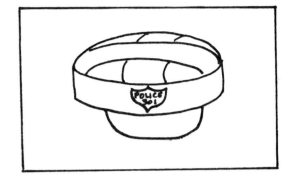

1. CUT OUT PATTERNS.
2. TRACE PATTERN "A" ON BLUE PAPER. CUT OUT. DRAW LINE AS SHOWN.
3. TRACE PATTERN "B" ON BLUE PAPER. CUT OUT. TWO.
4. CROSS TWO "B" & STAPLE IN CENTER - DIAGRAM #1.
5. CUT STRIP 1 ¾" X 6". STAPLE TO PATTERN "A." FIT TO HEAD.
6. STAPLE "B" UNIT TO FRONT, BACK & BOTH SIDES OF "A" UNIT.
7. TRACE BADGE ON YELLOW PAPER. CUT OUT. WRITE POLICE ON BADGE.
8. GLUE BADGE ON FRONT OF HAT.

POLICE BADGE
(YELLOW)
CUT 1

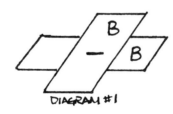

DIAGRAM #1

OPTIONS:
POLICE HAT - BLUE
SOLDIER HAT - GREEN
BUS DRIVER HAT - GRAY
POSTMAN HAT - BLUE

POLICEMAN HAT
(BLUE)
PATTERN "B"
CUT 2

CENTER STAPLE
FOR CROSS/UNIT B

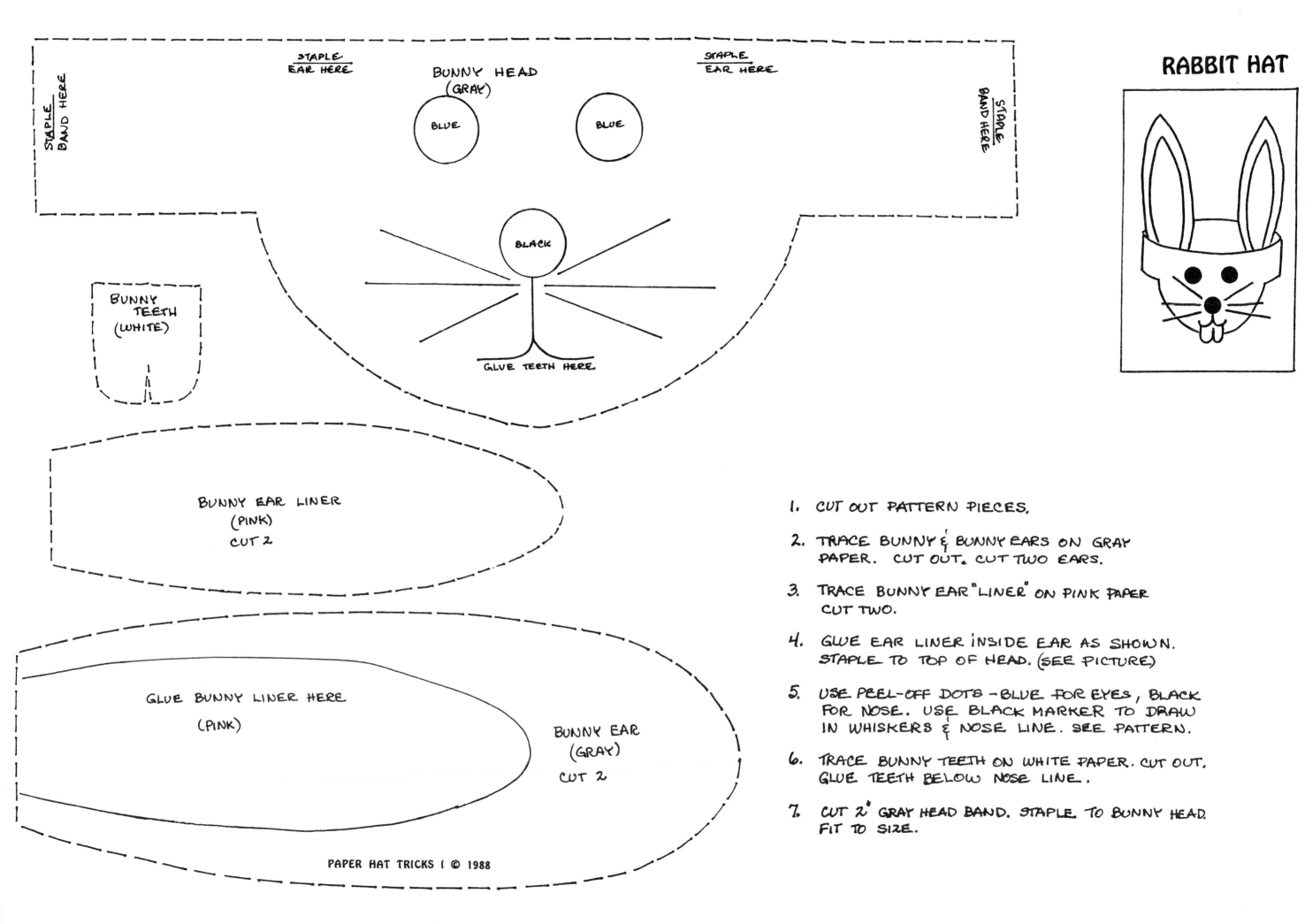

STAPLE BAND HERE

STAPLE EAR HERE

STAPLE EAR HERE

BUNNY HEAD
(GRAY)

BLUE

BLUE

BLACK

STAPLE BAND HERE

RABBIT HAT

BUNNY
TEETH
(WHITE)

GLUE TEETH HERE

BUNNY EAR LINER
(PINK)
CUT 2

GLUE BUNNY LINER HERE

(PINK)

BUNNY EAR
(GRAY)
CUT 2

1. CUT OUT PATTERN PIECES.

2. TRACE BUNNY & BUNNY EARS ON GRAY PAPER. CUT OUT. CUT TWO EARS.

3. TRACE BUNNY EAR "LINER" ON PINK PAPER CUT TWO.

4. GLUE EAR LINER INSIDE EAR AS SHOWN. STAPLE TO TOP OF HEAD. (SEE PICTURE)

5. USE PEEL-OFF DOTS – BLUE FOR EYES, BLACK FOR NOSE. USE BLACK MARKER TO DRAW IN WHISKERS & NOSE LINE. SEE PATTERN.

6. TRACE BUNNY TEETH ON WHITE PAPER. CUT OUT. GLUE TEETH BELOW NOSE LINE.

7. CUT 2" GRAY HEAD BAND. STAPLE TO BUNNY HEAD. FIT TO SIZE.

PAPER HAT TRICKS I © 1988

28

REINDEER HAT

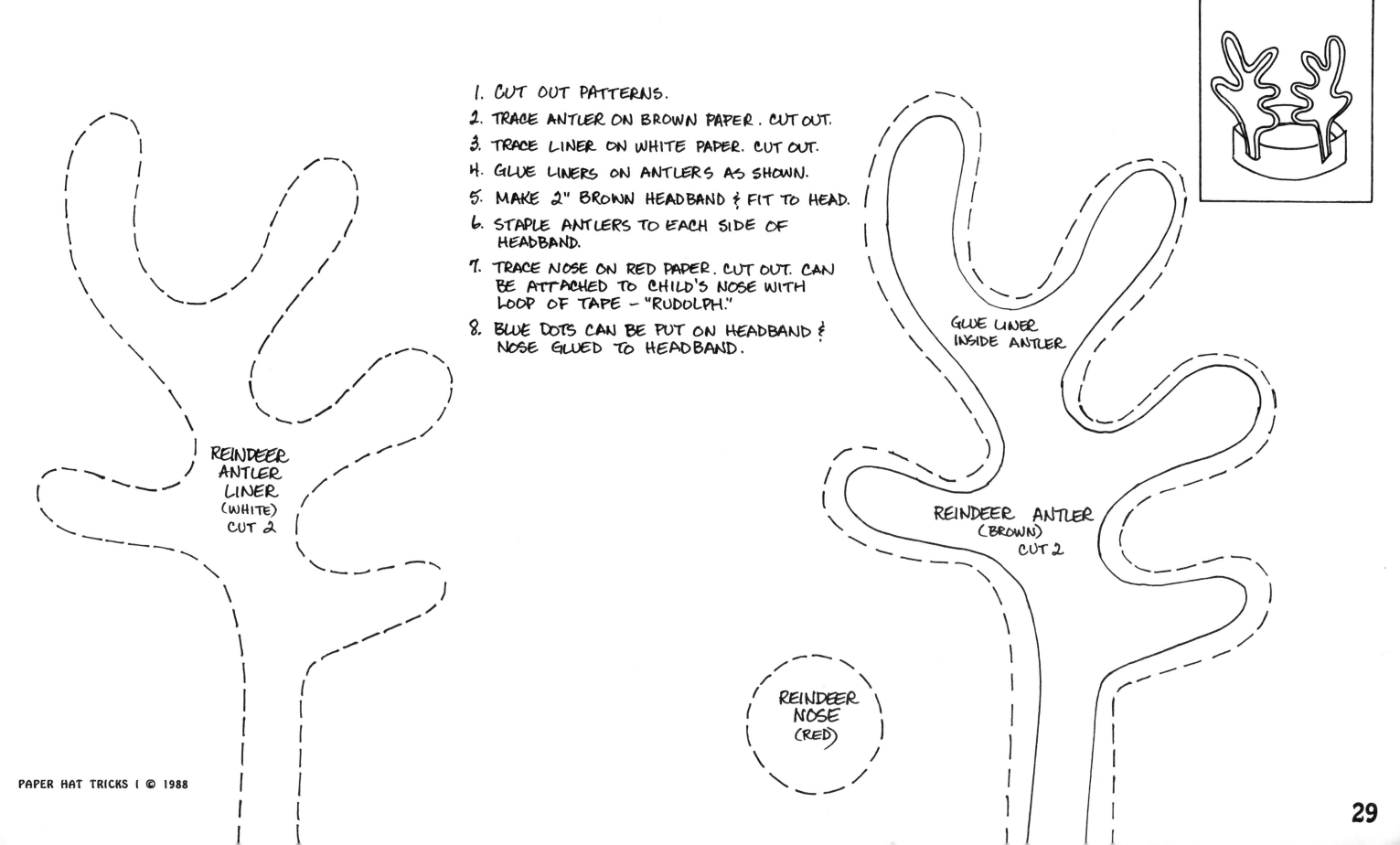

1. CUT OUT PATTERNS.
2. TRACE ANTLER ON BROWN PAPER. CUT OUT.
3. TRACE LINER ON WHITE PAPER. CUT OUT.
4. GLUE LINERS ON ANTLERS AS SHOWN.
5. MAKE 2" BROWN HEADBAND & FIT TO HEAD.
6. STAPLE ANTLERS TO EACH SIDE OF HEADBAND.
7. TRACE NOSE ON RED PAPER. CUT OUT. CAN BE ATTACHED TO CHILD'S NOSE WITH LOOP OF TAPE – "RUDOLPH."
8. BLUE DOTS CAN BE PUT ON HEADBAND & NOSE GLUED TO HEADBAND.

REINDEER ANTLER LINER (WHITE) CUT 2

GLUE LINER INSIDE ANTLER

REINDEER ANTLER (BROWN) CUT 2

REINDEER NOSE (RED)

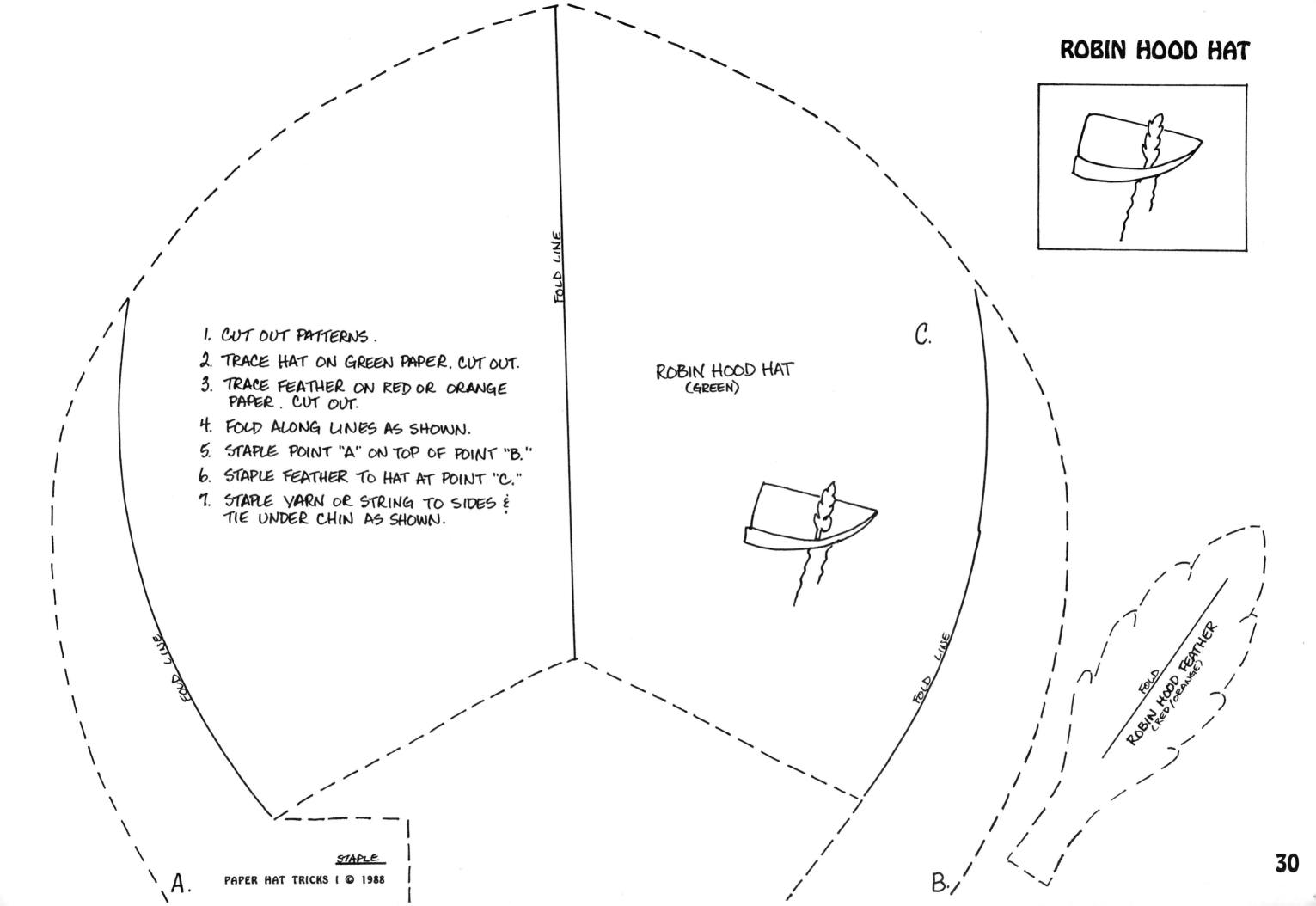

ROBIN HOOD HAT

1. CUT OUT PATTERNS.
2. TRACE HAT ON GREEN PAPER. CUT OUT.
3. TRACE FEATHER ON RED OR ORANGE PAPER. CUT OUT.
4. FOLD ALONG LINES AS SHOWN.
5. STAPLE POINT "A" ON TOP OF POINT "B."
6. STAPLE FEATHER TO HAT AT POINT "C."
7. STAPLE YARN OR STRING TO SIDES & TIE UNDER CHIN AS SHOWN.

FOLD LINE

ROBIN HOOD HAT
(GREEN)

C.

FOLD LINE

FOLD LINE

FOLD
ROBIN HOOD FEATHER
(RED/ORANGE)

STAPLE

A.

PAPER HAT TRICKS I © 1988

B.

30

SANTA CLAUS HAT

L

R

X GLUE COTTON BALL HERE

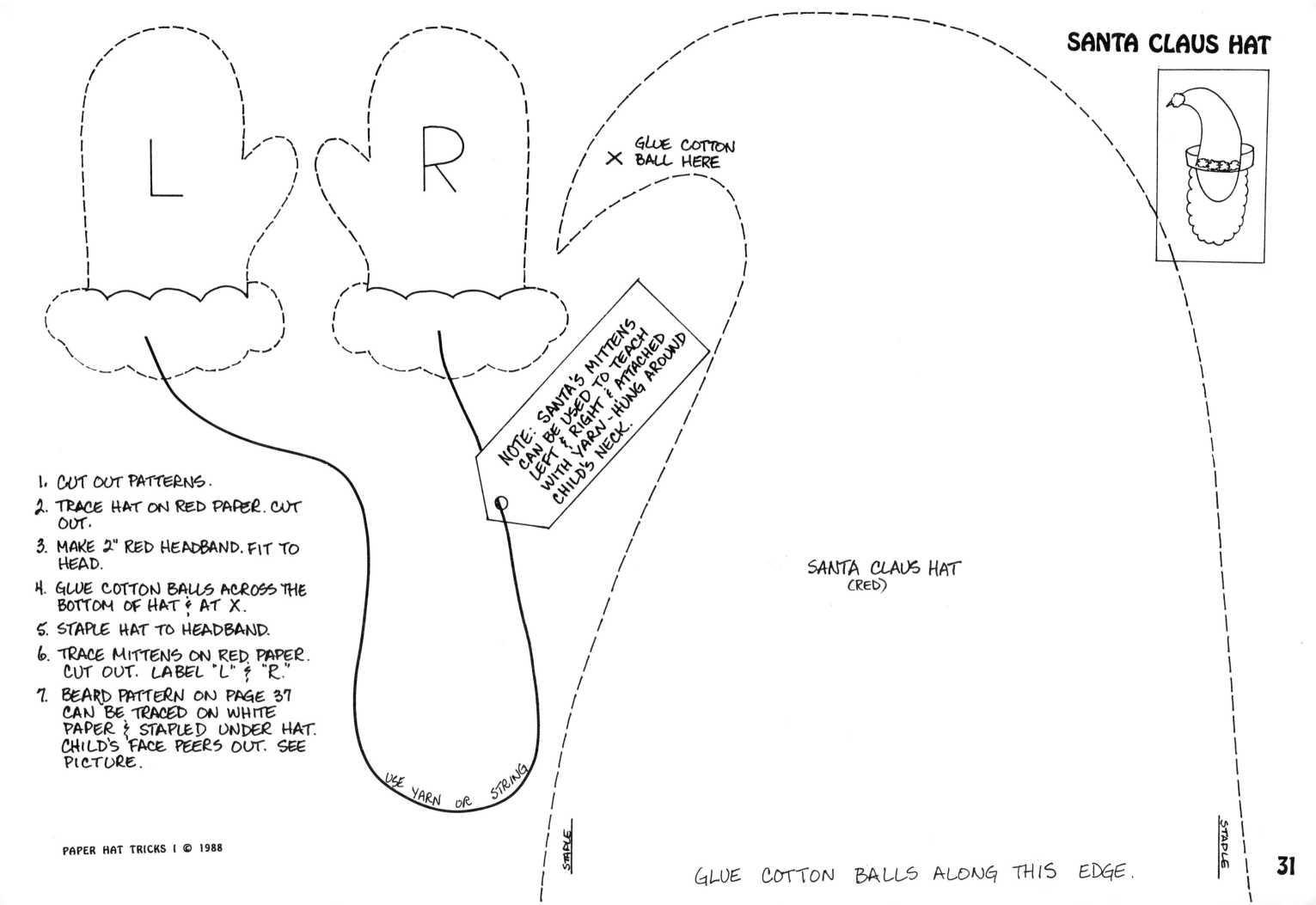

NOTE: SANTA'S MITTENS CAN BE USED TO TEACH LEFT & RIGHT & ATTACHED WITH YARN - HUNG AROUND CHILD'S NECK.

1. CUT OUT PATTERNS.

2. TRACE HAT ON RED PAPER. CUT OUT.

3. MAKE 2" RED HEADBAND. FIT TO HEAD.

4. GLUE COTTON BALLS ACROSS THE BOTTOM OF HAT & AT X.

5. STAPLE HAT TO HEADBAND.

6. TRACE MITTENS ON RED PAPER. CUT OUT. LABEL "L" & "R."

7. BEARD PATTERN ON PAGE 37 CAN BE TRACED ON WHITE PAPER & STAPLED UNDER HAT. CHILD'S FACE PEERS OUT. SEE PICTURE.

USE YARN OR STRING

SANTA CLAUS HAT
(RED)

STAPLE

STAPLE

GLUE COTTON BALLS ALONG THIS EDGE.

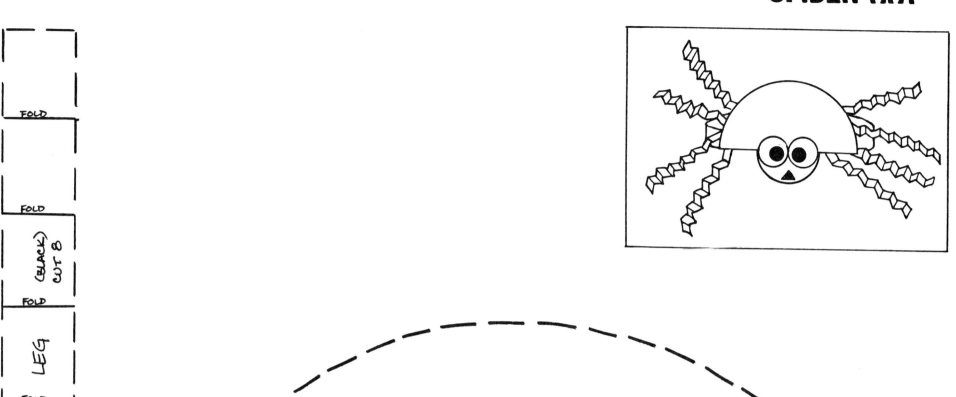

1. CUT OUT PATTERNS.
2. TRACE BODY & LEGS ON BLACK PAPER, CUT OUT. ACCORDIAN FOLD LEGS.
3. STAPLE 3 LEGS AT B & C AS SHOWN.
4. STAPLE 1 LEG AT D & E AS SHOWN.
5. USE WHITE & ORANGE DOTS FOR EYES AS SHOWN.
6. TRACE NOSE ON ORANGE PAPER, CUT OUT. GLUE AS SHOWN.
7. CUT 2" BLACK HEADBAND, FIT TO HEAD.
8. STAPLE SPIDER TO HEADBAND OVER EYES TO MAKE EYEBROWS AS SHOWN.

FOLD
FOLD
(BLACK) CUT 8
FOLD
LEG
SPIDER
FOLD
FOLD
FOLD
FOLD
FOLD

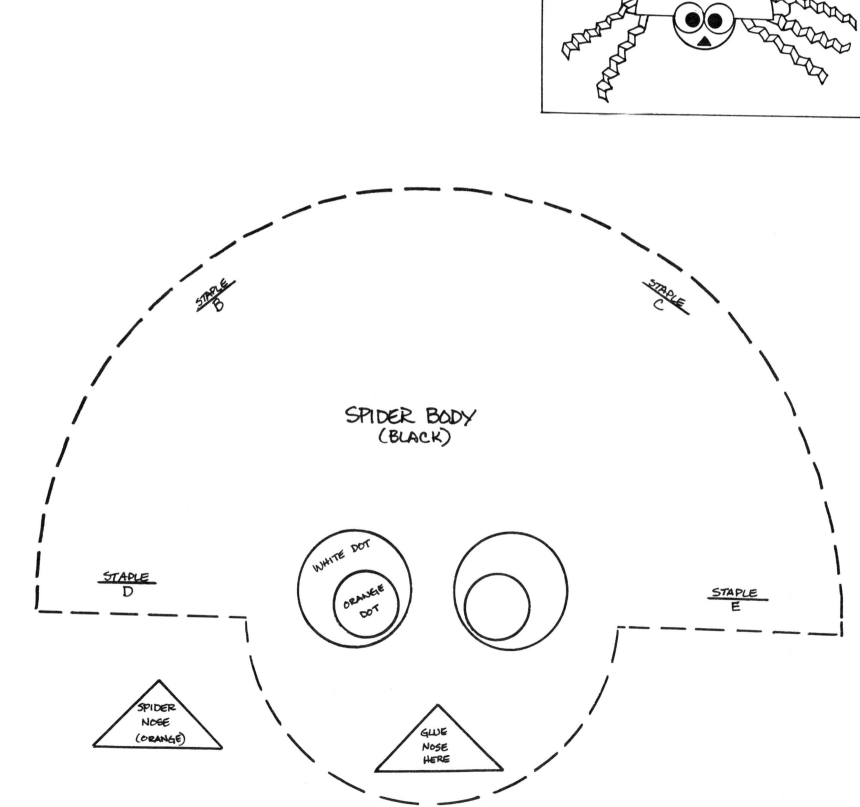

STAPLE B

STAPLE C

SPIDER BODY
(BLACK)

STAPLE D

WHITE DOT

ORANGE DOT

STAPLE E

SPIDER NOSE (ORANGE)

GLUE NOSE HERE

STATUE OF LIBERTY HAT

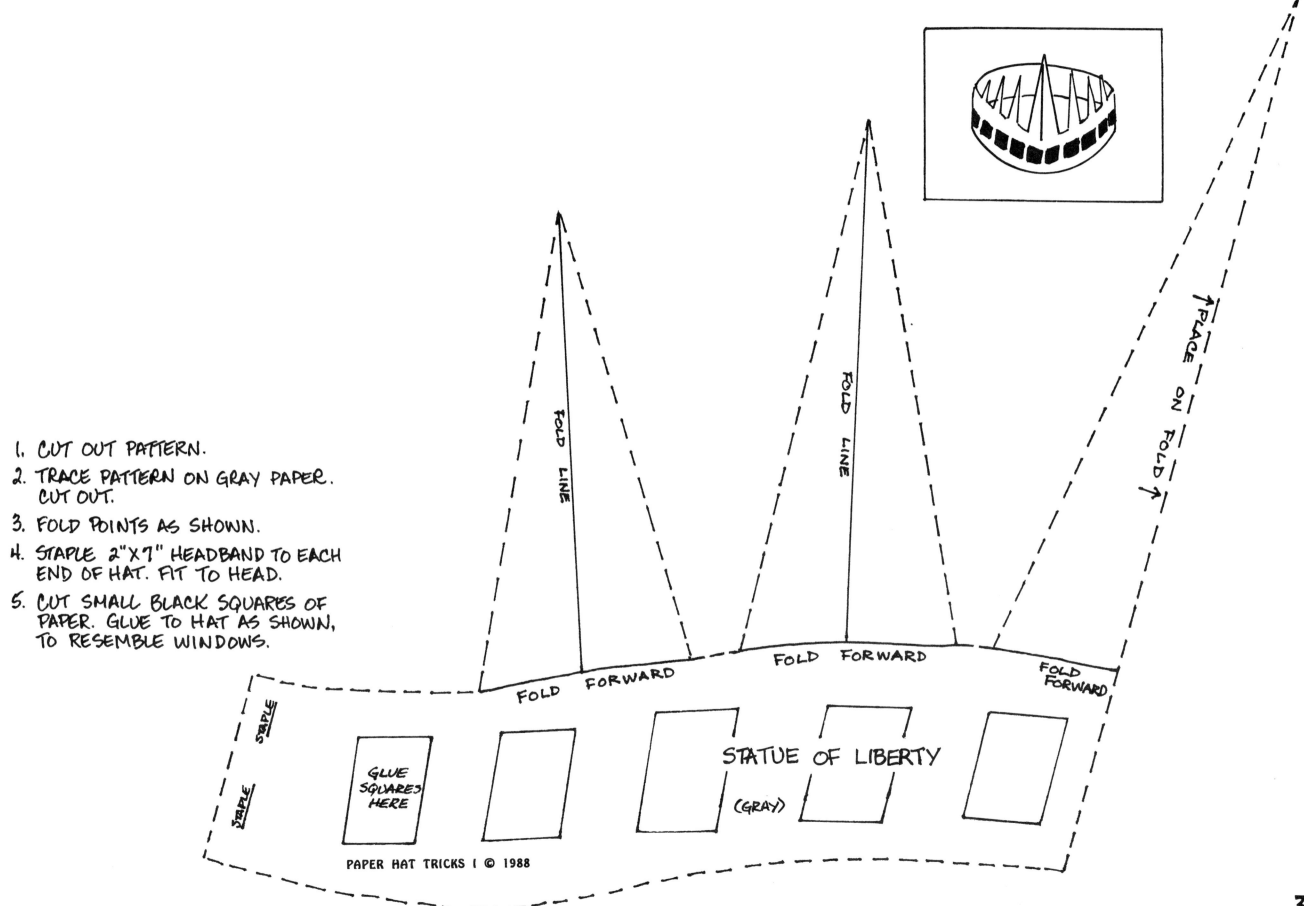

1. CUT OUT PATTERN.
2. TRACE PATTERN ON GRAY PAPER. CUT OUT.
3. FOLD POINTS AS SHOWN.
4. STAPLE 2"X 7" HEADBAND TO EACH END OF HAT. FIT TO HEAD.
5. CUT SMALL BLACK SQUARES OF PAPER. GLUE TO HAT AS SHOWN, TO RESEMBLE WINDOWS.

FOLD LINE

FOLD LINE

PLACE ON FOLD

FOLD FORWARD

FOLD FORWARD

FOLD FORWARD

STAPLE

STAPLE

GLUE SQUARES HERE

STATUE OF LIBERTY

(GRAY)

PAPER HAT TRICKS I © 1988

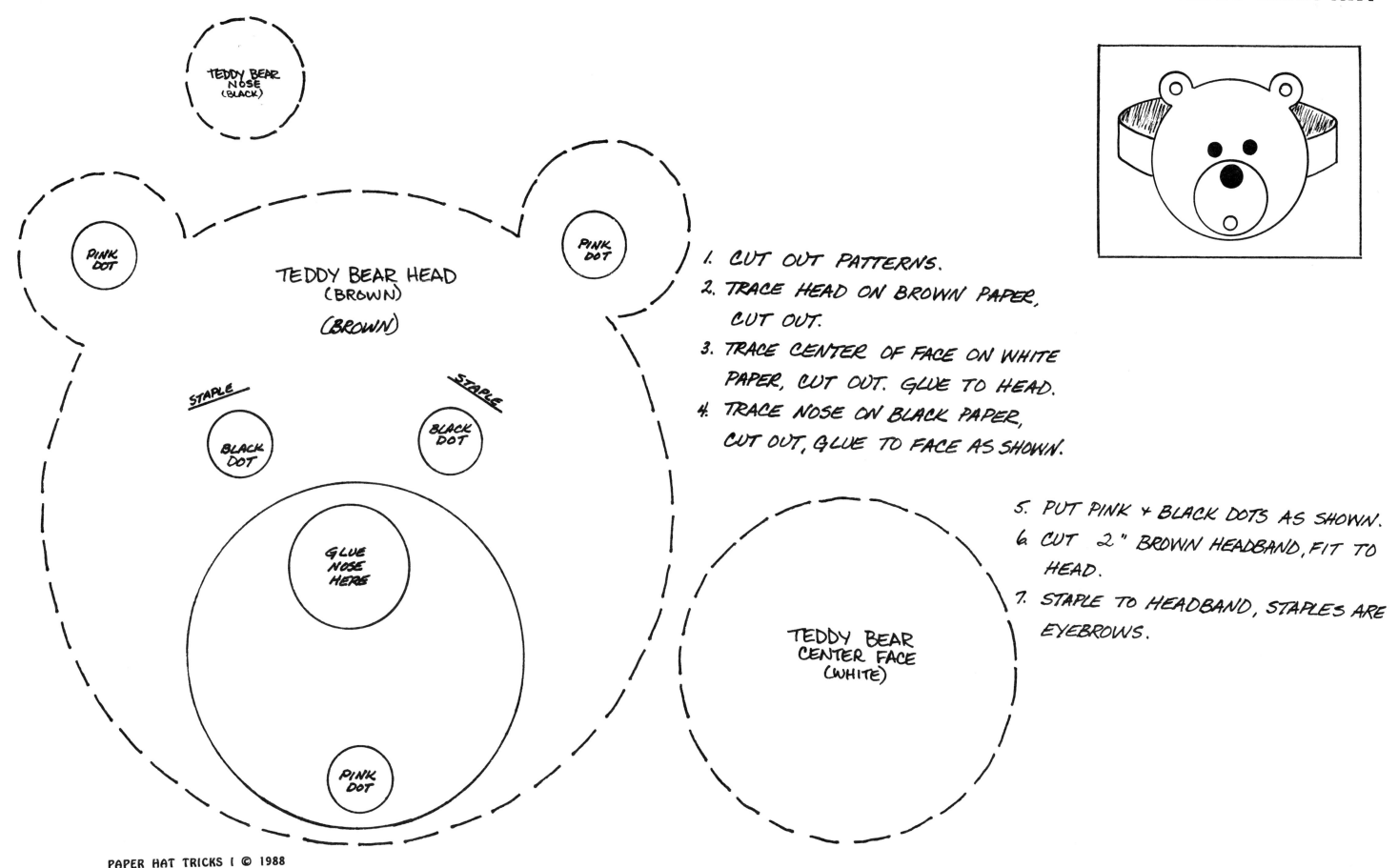

TEDDY BEAR HAT

TEDDY BEAR NOSE (BLACK)

TEDDY BEAR HEAD (BROWN)

(BROWN)

PINK DOT

PINK DOT

STAPLE

STAPLE

BLACK DOT

BLACK DOT

GLUE NOSE HERE

PINK DOT

TEDDY BEAR CENTER FACE (WHITE)

1. CUT OUT PATTERNS.
2. TRACE HEAD ON BROWN PAPER, CUT OUT.
3. TRACE CENTER OF FACE ON WHITE PAPER, CUT OUT. GLUE TO HEAD.
4. TRACE NOSE ON BLACK PAPER, CUT OUT, GLUE TO FACE AS SHOWN.

5. PUT PINK & BLACK DOTS AS SHOWN.
6. CUT 2" BROWN HEADBAND, FIT TO HEAD.
7. STAPLE TO HEADBAND, STAPLES ARE EYEBROWS.

1. CUT OUT PATTERN.
2. TRACE HAT ON BLUE PAPER. CUT OUT.
3. DRAW WHITE LINES WITH CHALK OR WHITE CRAYON ON HAT & LARGE BLUE NAPKIN.
4. CREASE FOLD LINES TO MAKE BILL, STAPLE IF NECESSARY.
5. STAPLE 3" BLUE HEADBAND TO ONE END. FIT TO HEAD. STAPLE OTHER END.
6. TUCK CORNERS OF NAPKINS EVENLY AROUND HEADBAND & HAT. STAPLE TO MAKE GATHERS.
7. PUFF TOP OF NAPKIN AS SHOWN.
8. TIE RED BANDANA AROUND NECK.

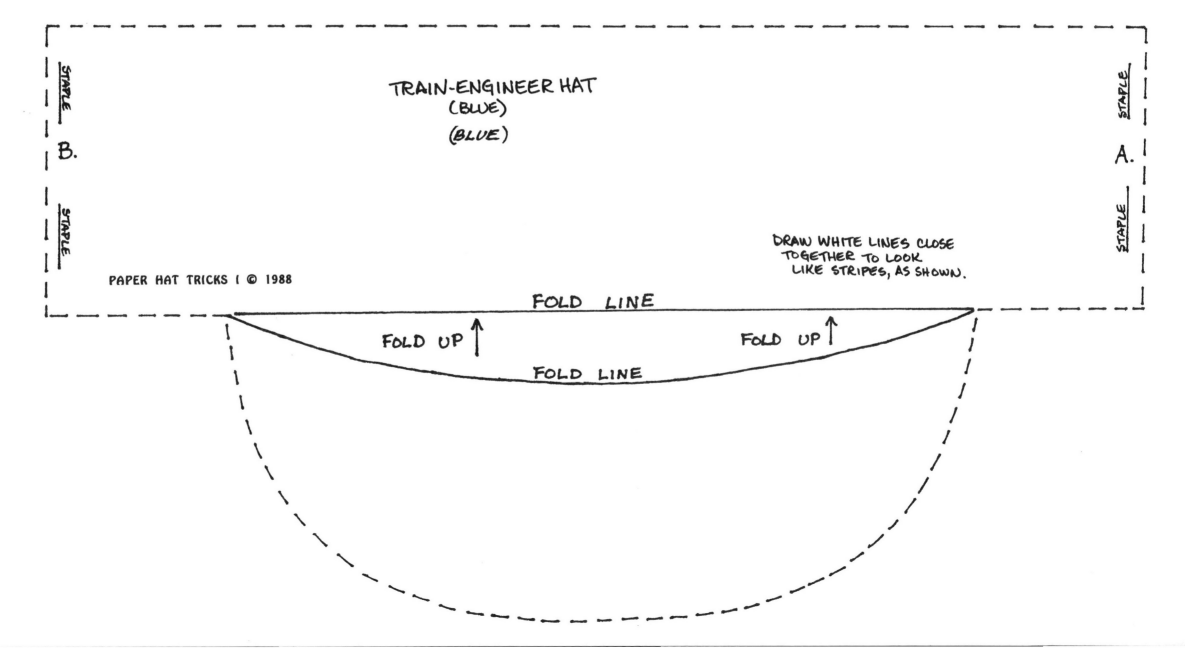

STAPLE B.

TRAIN-ENGINEER HAT
(BLUE)

(BLUE)

STAPLE A.

STAPLE

PAPER HAT TRICKS I © 1988

DRAW WHITE LINES CLOSE TOGETHER TO LOOK LIKE STRIPES, AS SHOWN.

FOLD LINE

FOLD UP ↑   FOLD UP ↑

FOLD LINE

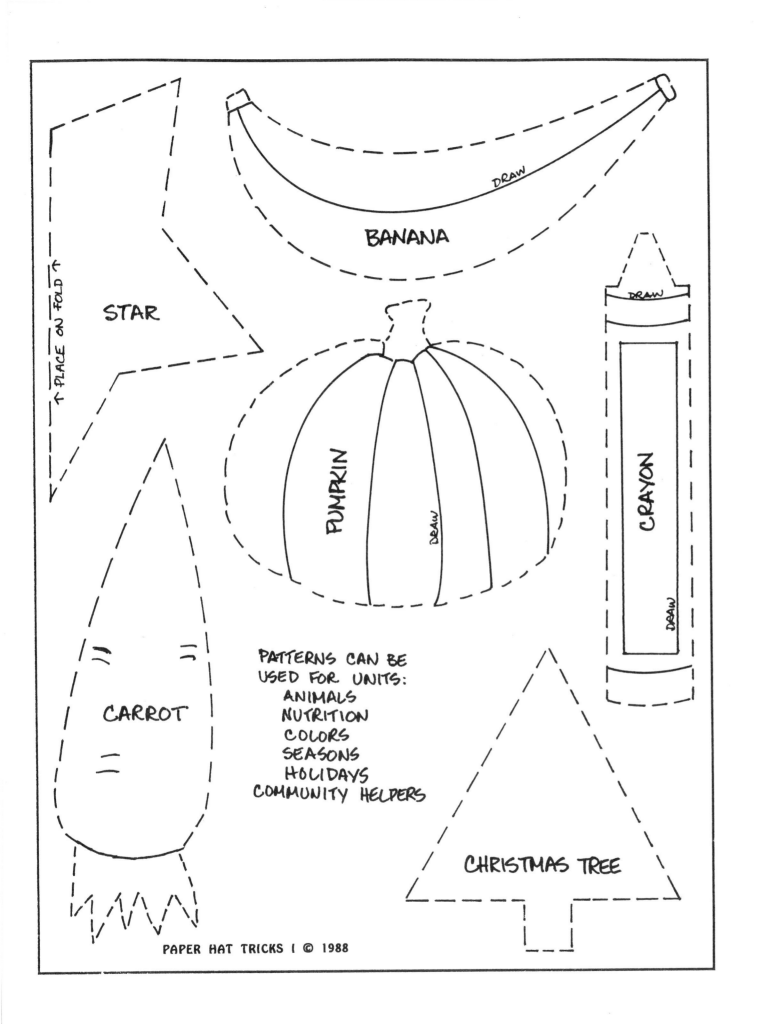

STAR

↑ PLACE ON FOLD ↑

BANANA

DRAW

PUMPKIN

DRAW

CRAYON

DRAW

DRAW

CARROT

PATTERNS CAN BE
USED FOR UNITS:
  ANIMALS
  NUTRITION
  COLORS
  SEASONS
  HOLIDAYS
COMMUNITY HELPERS

CHRISTMAS TREE

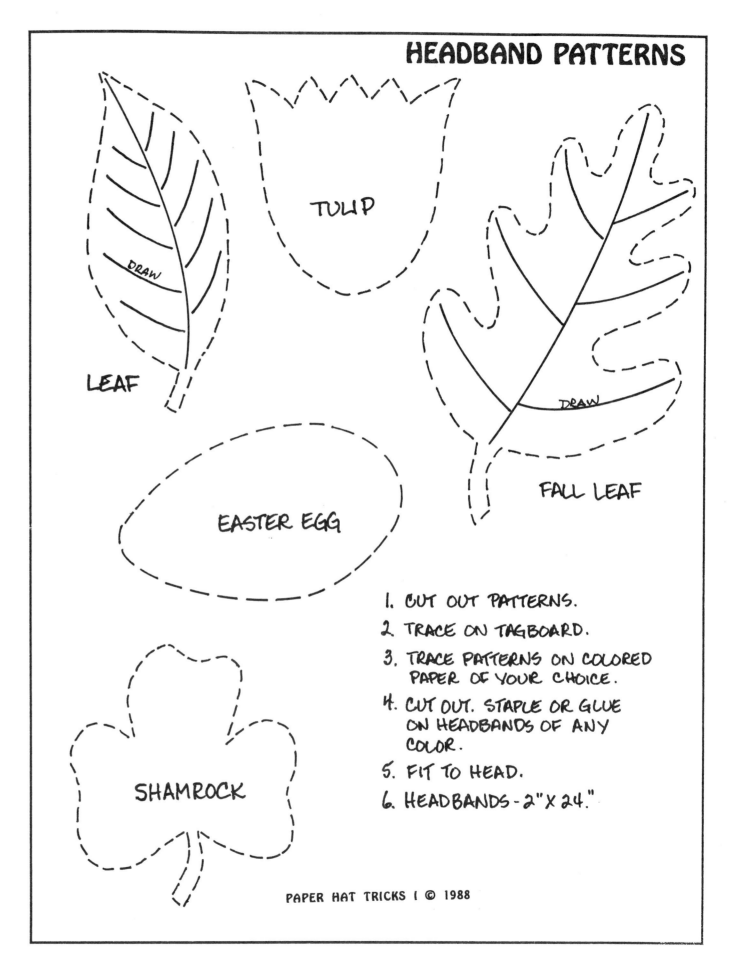

HEADBAND PATTERNS

TULIP

LEAF

DRAW

FALL LEAF

DRAW

EASTER EGG

SHAMROCK

1. CUT OUT PATTERNS.
2. TRACE ON TAGBOARD.
3. TRACE PATTERNS ON COLORED PAPER OF YOUR CHOICE.
4. CUT OUT. STAPLE OR GLUE ON HEADBANDS OF ANY COLOR.
5. FIT TO HEAD.
6. HEADBANDS - 2" X 24."

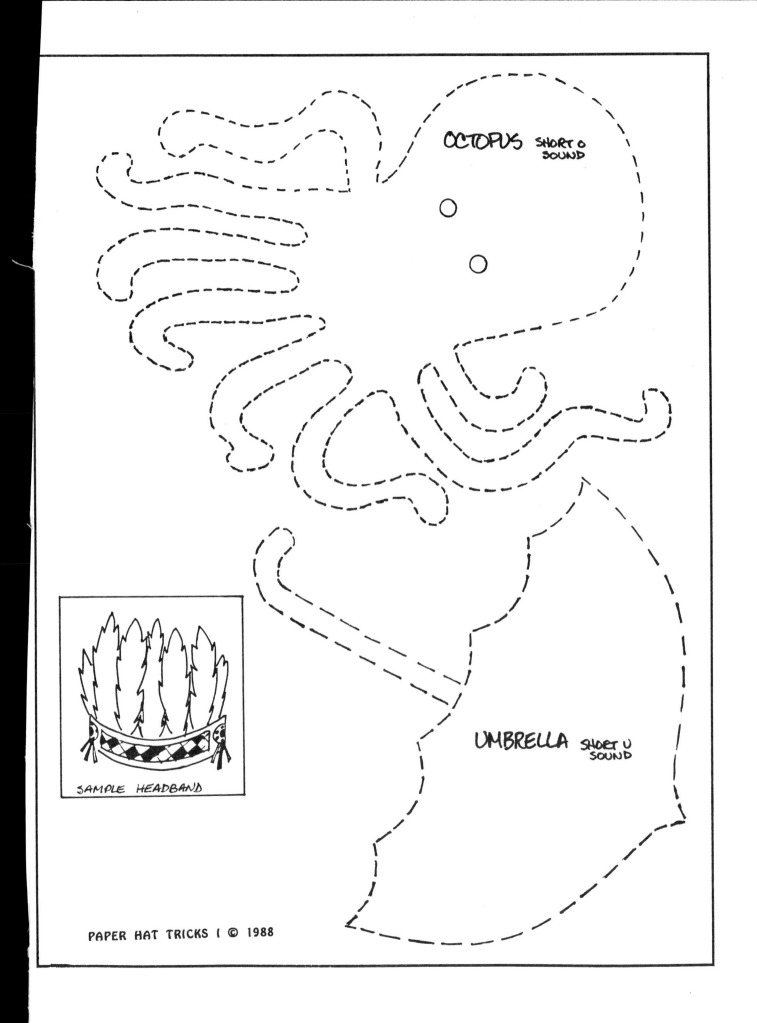

OCTOPUS SHORT O SOUND

SAMPLE HEADBAND

UMBRELLA SHORT U SOUND

PAPER HAT TRICKS I © 1988

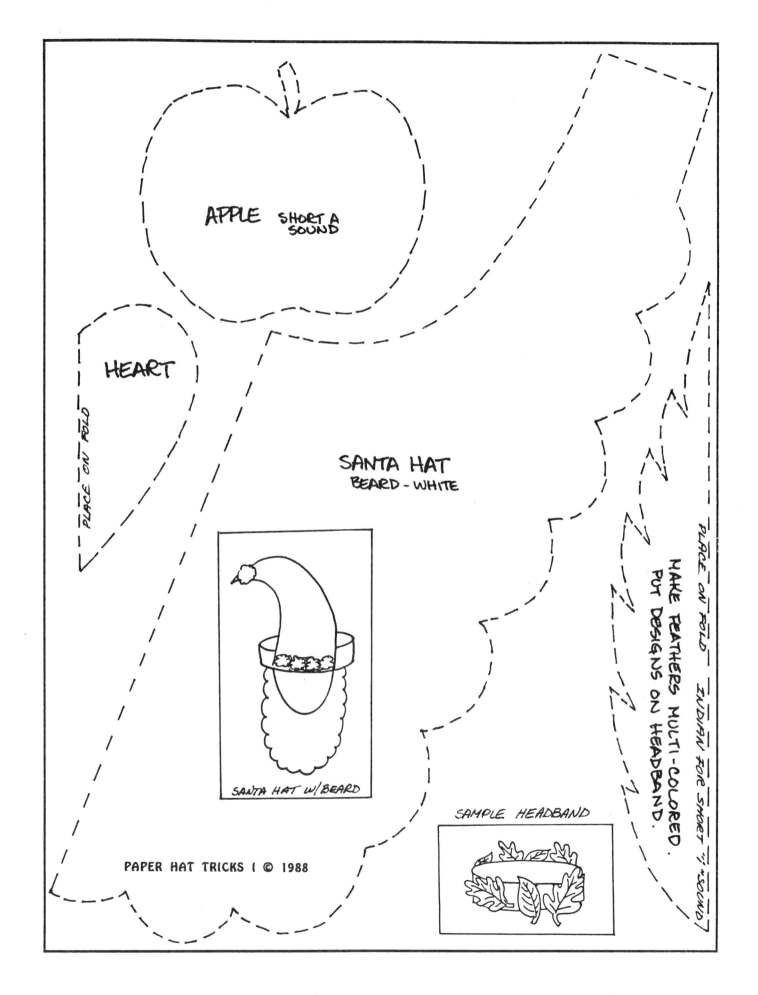

APPLE SHORT A SOUND

HEART

PLACE ON FOLD

SANTA HAT
BEARD - WHITE

SANTA HAT W/BEARD

PAPER HAT TRICKS I © 1988

SAMPLE HEADBAND

PLACE ON FOLD   INDIAN FOR SHORT "I" SOUND

MAKE FEATHERS MULTI-COLORED.
PUT DESIGNS ON HEADBAND.